E

MW00777083

THE MAYOR OF CASTERBRIDGE
BY
THOMAS HARDY

Intelligent Education

INFLUENCE
PUBLISHERS

Nashville, Tennessee

BRIGHT NOTES: The Mayor of Casterbridge
www.BrightNotes.com

ISBN: 978-1-645424-90-1 (Paperback)
ISBN: 978-1-645424-91-8 (eBook)

Published in accordance with the U.S. Copyright Office Orphan Works and Mass Digitization report of the register of copyrights, June 2015.

Originally published by Monarch Press.
Ken Sobel, 1964
2019 Edition published by Influence Publishers.

Interior design by Lapiz Digital Services. Cover Design by Thinkpen Designs.

Printed in the United States of America.

Library of Congress Cataloging-in-Publication Data forthcoming.
Names: Intelligent Education
Title: BRIGHT NOTES: The Mayor of Casterbridge
Subject: STU004000 STUDY AIDS / Book Notes

CONTENTS

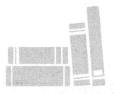

LIFE OF HARDY

Thomas Hardy, the son of a building contractor, was born in 1840 in a small town in Dorset, in southwestern England. He attended church regularly with his family, and later taught in the local Sunday school. As a boy he memorized all the services, and this knowledge underlies the frequent references to religion in his works. In addition, Thomas' father was a musician who played at church services, and the boy followed in his father's footsteps by learning to play the violin. This was the start of a lifelong interest in music, which also figures prominently in his books. Although young Hardy's education was not particularly good, there were books in his home and he read all he could. At the age of sixteen, he left school and was apprenticed to an architect. Hardy is thus one of the relatively few well-known English writers who did not have a university education (Shakespeare and Dickens are others). Although his formal studies stopped, he continued to educate himself. He would arise early in the morning and study for an hour or two before leaving for work. In this way he continued to read various Latin and English authors and also taught himself Greek. In 1862 he left the architect's office, well trained as a draftsman and with a considerable amount of reading behind him. At the age of twenty-two he left Dorset for London. There young Hardy came into contact for the first time with the advances of the modern world. It must be understood that life in the Dorset of the 1840's and 1850's had hardly changed in its broad outlines since the Middle Ages. It was nearly completely rural in character, and at that time was still, sufficiently isolated from the rest of the world for few of the industrial and mechanical aspects of modem civilization to have come to it. (Dorset provides the setting for most of Hardy's novels and stories, including those that are generally thought to be his best. Hardy, however, changed the name of Dorset to "Wessex," and he changed the names of all the towns he wrote of as well. A map of the Wessex country, with both the real and fictional names of the places that occur in Hardy's work, is to be found in the edition of *Tess of the d'Urbervilles* edited by Carl J. Weber—see Bibliography.) In London he worked as an architect. He also studied French, visited art galleries and the great London exposition, and continued his course of reading. During these years he wrote the first of his poems to survive. It is clear that he greatly expanded his mental horizons, but he paid a price for his excessive exertions—his health suffered and he was generally unhappy. In 1867 he returned to Dorset, but not as a full-time architect. He temporarily stopped writing poetry and made his first attempt at prose fiction. Hardy had reached a real crossroads in his life. By 1868 he had completed his first novel—*The Poor Man and the Lady*—which, though it was rejected, convinced him that he should continue his efforts at novel-writing. In the same year he did his last work as an architect, and it was during this time that he met the girl he was to marry. It was altogether a most crucial year for Hardy.

HIS NOVELS

Ail Hardy's novels were written during the next twenty-eight years. *The Poor Man and the Lady* was a slashing social satire, and when it was rejected Hardy switched to writing romances, stories with complicated plots and much sensational action. He began with *Desperate Remedies* in 1871, *Under the Greenwood Tree* (1872) and *A Pair of Blue Eyes* (1873). These books are highly autobiographical (as are the first novels of most writers), and they were reasonably well reviewed. *Under the Greenwood Tree* was the first of the novels to have a rural setting. Before *A Pair of Blue Eyes* appeared as a book, it came out as a serial in a magazine, and this set a pattern—nearly all the rest of Hardy's novels were first published in this form. (This was a common practice for novelists in general in the nineteenth century.) In 1874 he published *Far from the Madding Crowd,* the earliest of the novels which are generally read today. This book received very favorable reviews, and Hardy followed it with *The Hand of Ethelberta* in 1876. The latter work is not a pastoral novel because Hardy decided that he did not want to be identified in the public mind as a writer who could only write about "cows and sheep." Throughout his novel-writing career Hardy was very sensitive to the reading public, and he often acknowledged that he sought popularity. The next book Hardy composed is certainly among his best and most popular— *The Return of the Native* (1878). This was followed by several volumes which are not among his most successful efforts: *The Trumpet-Major* (1880), *A Laodicean* A 1881), and *Two on a Tower* (1882). By this time Hardy was recognized to be one of England's leading novelists, and this reputation was greatly enhanced by the books that appeared in the next decade. This period of Hardy's career saw the production of those novels that have ensured him lasting fame. In 1886 there was *The Mayor of Casterbridge,* in 1887 *The Woodlanders;* 1891 saw *Tess of the d'Urbervilles,* and *Jude the Obscure,* the last novel he wrote, appeared in 1896. (*The Well-Beloved* came out in 1897, but it had been written in 1892.) Throughout these years Hardy was composing short stories as well as novels, and several volumes of these stories appeared, as follows: *Wessex Tales* (1888), *A Group of Noble Dames* (1891), and *Life's Little Ironies* (1894). (A last book of stories, *A Changed Man, The Waiting Supper, and Other Tales,* came out much later, in 1913.) After *Jude the Obscure* Hardy mainly wrote poetry. It should be remembered that he started out as a poet and had been composing poetry throughout the time he was writing novels. The last novels he published were all very controversial, and they caused Hardy to undergo some very severe criticism. This criticism, which sometimes amounted to personal abuse, combined with his continuing love for poetry and his newly won financial security, caused him to abandon the novel and return to poetry. *Wessex Poems*, which contained some of his earliest work, came out in 1898 and was received very well. In 1901 he published *Poems of the Past and Present.* The first part of his great epic poem *The Dynasts* appeared in 1903. It deals with the Napoleonic Wars and is one of the longest poems in English. The second and third parts came out in 1906 and 1908. The satirical title of *Time's Laughing-Stocks* (1909) indicates something of the bitter tone of this collection of ballad-like poems about sexual infidelity and unsuccessful marriage. It is thought that Hardy's own marriage was not especially happy, but its tensions were not to last much longer. In 1912 his wife Emma died. Hardy expressed his deep feeling for her in several of the poems that made up his next collection of verse: *Satires of Circumstance, Lyrics and Reveries* (1914). Hardy was then seventy-two, and the loss of his wife was a great shock. His life seemed to disintegrate, and he passed through two disastrous, disorganized years. In 1914, however, he married again, and his life once more regained its balance. In the same year the First World War broke out, but it did not check his inspiration. He continued to write, and in 1917 brought out *Moments of Vision and Miscellaneous Verses.* He followed this by *Late Lyrics and Earlier* (1922), the verse drama *The Queen of Cornwall* (1923), *Human Shows* (1925), and finally *Winter Words,* published posthumously in the year of his death, 1928.

HARDY'S TIME

The age in which Hardy wrote, sometimes called the late Victorian period (after Queen Victoria, who reigned from 1837 to 1901), was one of great change and many difficulties. In fact, in the Victorian period we can see the beginnings of many of the problems of our own time. English society was experiencing severe strains in its attempts to adjust to vast alterations in its structure, and *Tess of the d'Urbervilles* reflects its author's concern with several of the most pressing problems of his time. Hardy depicts the effects of the pressure of the new, urban, and industrial civilization on the old, rural, and agricultural life of Wessex. He exposes the hypocrisy of the rules that govern sexual behavior and the position of women in society. The third leading theme of the book is the question, especially acute in his day, of how to live in a time when religion no longer provided acceptable rules of conduct. Both Angel and Alec are typical young men of the age, sufficiently enlightened to reject the traditional standards, but unable to create new ones for themselves. Thus both are alone in relation to their society. *Tess* is one of the first novels to examine this theme (a major one ever since) of the effects of spiritual and moral isolation in modem society. Of course *Tess* is a novel and not a textbook on morals, and therefore these problems are not taken up in a systematic way; rather, they form the background of ideas and feelings against which the characters move and act.

THE NOVEL'S STRUCTURE

The structure of the novel has often been discussed. Thomas Hardy was an architect by training, and it is tempting to suppose that this background may have caused him to plan his novels as carefully as we know he did. Before he began to write, he worked out a detailed outline, including a table of important dates in the lives of his characters (for such a table on *Tess,* see the appendix of Weber's *Hardy of Wessex*). In the past Hardy's structural craftsmanship has often been praised, but today opinion has changed. Present-day critics still believe that a novel requires careful planning and construction, but they now think that the reader should not be aware of the craftsman at work. In Hardy, the reader is all too often conscious of the details of the structure (it is as if one were aware of all the carpentry in a house). Take, for instance, the rather mechanical alternation between spring and fall, and the fact that Tess is arrested at Stonehenge on June 1, just five years to the day that she set out to visit Trantridge. Nevertheless, if we do sometimes see the puppeteer a little too clearly behind the stage, there is no denying the cumulative power and effect of the tragedy that befalls Tess, and this is in large measure due to the careful plan of the book, obvious or not.

THE MAYOR OF CASTERBRIDGE

. . . .

THE MAYOR OF CASTERBRIDGE

Of all the Wessex novels, however, *The Mayor of Casterbridge*, published in 1886, is the least typical. It makes much less use of the physical environment than do the others although of course it does not ignore it. Undoubtedly, the fact that it takes place primarily in a town accounts for this. Casterbridge, which is modeled very closely on Dorchester, while still dependent on farming, is somewhat more sophisticated than the surrounding countryside. It has a clearly defined social structure, symbolized by the three inns which the different classes frequent. In addition, it is a main stopping point along the Great West Road and on a main north-south artery as well. This gives Casterbridge a certain eminence in Wessex.

Partly because of the relative importance of Casterbridge, much of the regional color found in the other novels is lacking. Some is still present but the chorus, for example, really has little to do in *The Mayor of Casterbridge*. There is also little emphasis plated upon manual labor, in contrast to the other novels. Most of the important characters are townbred, and all live on their inherited wealth or business acumen. Of all of them, Henchard is the only one who knows what it is to work in the fields.

ITS OUTSTANDING FEATURE

These are all minor differences however. By far the outstanding feature that makes *The Mayor of Casterbridge* unique is its single-minded concentration upon one central character. The other figures in the book hardly matter. Only Elizabeth-Jane seems to have any independent life outside of her association with Henchard, and she not very much. Henchard dominates the action at every turn. We learn about the town mainly in relation to his activities in it. There is a minimum of extra description and comment, at least for Hardy.

BRIEF SUMMARY OF THE PLOT

The novel begins with the most sensational incident in the entire story: Henchard's drunken sale of his wife Susan and their infant daughter to a passing sailor. As in a Greek tragedy, this first crime sets off a series of others. We know that this pattern will eventually end in disaster for the original perpetrator. Henchard has sealed his fate in the first two chapters. The remainder of the novel relates the inevitable unfolding of that fate.

His downfall begins almost twenty years after his crime. In the interim, Henchard has reached great heights of fortune. He has risen from a fieldhand to Mayor of Casterbridge. We learn that it is precisely because of his misdeed, because of the lesson it taught him about disciplining himself, that he has made his way in the world. He no longer drinks and he controls his temper so that his natural abilities have come out.

Susan's return with Elizabeth-Jane, after the reported shipwreck of the sailor, coincides with the arrival of Donald Farfrae. Farfrae does Henchard a great favor which helps him in his grain dealing business. Henchard is so impressed that he prevails upon the young Scot to remain in Casterbridge as his manager. At the same time, driven by guilt feelings, he "remarries" Susan and brings her and Elizabeth-Jane, now a young woman, into his house. These two acts set in motion the inevitable workings of fate. It is noteworthy that Henchard himself brings them about. "Character is fate," Hardy says. We begin to see that it is Henchard's fate to be destroyed by his own impulsive, prideful character.

Farfrae proves himself an excellent businessman. He is so good, in fact, that Henchard becomes resentful. After a series of incidents, culminating in a too-successful party given by Farfrae, Henchard fires him. To Henchard's annoyance, Farfrae sets up a grain business of his own. Shortly afterward, Susan dies leaving a letter to be opened on her daughter's marriage day. Henchard opens it anyway and discovers to his horror that Elizabeth-Jane is not his daughter but the sailor's. His daughter had died soon after the sale. He becomes very cold toward her, making her life miserable.

A woman with whom he had an affair sometime before comes to reside in Casterbridge. Her name is "Lucetta Le Sueur." As her names indicates, she is foreign, seductive and somewhat immoral. She intends to marry Henchard. He has no objections since he had ruined her reputation and now feels he should make amends. Lucetta meets Elizabeth-Jane soon after her arrival, realizes that she is unhappy, and invites her to come to live in the house she has taken. She assumes that it is a good way to make Henchard's visits to her appear innocent to the townspeople.

Farfrae comes to court Elizabeth-Jane but meets Lucetta instead and is swept off his feet. They fall in love and Lucetta refuses to see Henchard although he is now anxious to marry her. He becomes furious and decides to crush Farfrae. In his blind determination, he makes a ruinous business deal and is bankrupted. He loses his house, his business, and all of his money. Almost at the same time, a woman who had witnessed the sale of his wife comes to the town. She is only too happy to reveal Henchard's past. He is immediately ruined socially as well.

Lucetta offers to help him financially but he discovers that she has secretly married Farfrae and refuses. She asks him to return some love letters she had written during their affair, of which Farfrae knows nothing. Henchard chivalrously agrees, giving them to his former manager to deliver. The manager, an unpleasant, vengeful man, bears a grudge against Lucetta, unknown to Henchard. He takes the letter of a dive where he and some of the town riff-raff open and read them for a joke. The next morning, he delivers them and Lucetta burns the package at once.

The local drifters and petty criminals decide to hold a skimmity-ride. This was a crude custom designed to humiliate a woman who had been unfaithful to her husband. An effigy of the adulterous pair is made and paraded around the town. Although Farfrae is sent out of town by some friends, Lucetta is wildly upset by the prank. She has an epileptic fit. Henchard, by accident, is the only person in town who knows where Farfrae has gone. He rushes to find him but, when he does, Farfrae will not trust his word and goes on his way. By the time he returns, Lucetta is near death. The next morning she is gone.

Henchard and Elizabeth-Jane become reconciled. Then, the sailor comes to Casterbridge looking for Susan and his daughter.

He explains that he was not drowned after all. Stunned, Henchard impulsively tells him they are both dead. The sailor departs immediately. Henchard is ashamed of his actions and chases after him but it is too late.

In the months that follow, Henchard finds some happiness living with Elizabeth-Jane in a small shop the town has set up for them. Soon, however, the sailor returns having learned the truth. Henchard leaves Casterbridge at once, miserable and ashamed, intending to go far away and subsist by hay-trussing in the fields, his original occupation. His love for Elizabeth-Jane makes it impossible for him to leave the region. Working about 50 miles away, he hears that she and Farfrae are getting married.

He resolves to go to the wedding reception, offers his apologies, and beg for forgiveness. She spurns him when he appears, however. He leaves for good without a further word. Soon afterward, he dies of a broken heart, alone and attended only by a feeble-minded former employee. Elizabeth-Jane relents and comes to find him, but by then it is too late. His tragedy has been certain since the opening chapters. Its working out is the essence of *The Mayor of Casterbridge*. But, if Henchard had not done such and such, one might object, he would have been saved. But what makes *The Mayor of Casterbridge* a great novel is precisely that Henchard's character is so constructed that he cannot react any way other than he does. Anyone else could and would have, but not Henchard. Nothing is really inevitable and yet everything is. This is the final conclusion of *The Mayor of Casterbridge*.

THE MAYOR OF CASTERBRIDGE

....

CHAPTER I

It is a warm, pleasant evening in the late summer of the year 1826. A young man and his wife, dusty from long travel, are walking along a country road toward the village of Weydon-Priors, in Upper Wessex, England. The woman is carrying their infant daughter. Although they are walking side by side, the two adults do not speak to each other. The man, in particular, seems disdainfully determined to ignore his traveling companions.

He walks proudly, holding himself firmly erect, never looking at the others. He is tall and impressively handsome with a stern, angular face. His complexion is dark from years of working in the fields.

His wife, on the other hand, is as ordinary looking as he is distinctive. Although she is somewhat pretty, in a tired way, her expression is dull and apathetic, as if she were resigned to a hard, oppressive life and no longer even cared what the future held for her.

Walking silently along the road, they encounter no one for quite a while. Finally, when they are already within sight of the outlying houses of Weydon-Priors, they meet a turnip-hoer returning home after the day's work. The young man stops him and asks if he knows of any work in the area for a hay trusser. The hoer points out with a sneer that it is the wrong time of year for such work. He goes on to say that Weydon-Priors is going through hard times and the hay trusser won't even be able to find a cottage for his family to live in. But, isn't there something going on today, the trusser asks, and the hoer informs him that today is Fair Day in Weydon-Priors, although he himself isn't fool enough to attend.

The trusser and his family continue on and soon come to the fair field. It is crowded with local people, some traders buying and selling livestock, but mostly holiday makers out for a good time at the peep-shows, toy stands, wax works, freak exhibits, and all the other common features of a fair. The travelers, however, are tired and only interested in finding a refreshment tent. As they look around, they see two close at hand. One advertises "Good, Home-brewed Beer, Ale and Cyder." The other has a placard in front reading "Good Furmity Sold Hear:

The man inclines to the beer tent, but his wife begs that they have furmity (see Glossary) instead and he gives in. The furmity tent is jammed. An old hag-like woman presides behind the counter and from her they order basins of hot furmity. The man soon discovers that, for an extra fee, the old hag will lace the furmity with rum. He guiltily tries to conceal the addition from his wife but she notices However, she says nothing.

He finishes the first basin and orders another with an ever larger proportion of rum. His wife protests but he does not listen. Becoming more and more drunk, he begins to argue vociferously with those around him. After his fourth basin, the discussion turns to the ruin of good men by bad wives and he remarks bitterly. "I married at eighteen like the fool I was; and this is the consequence o't." He points resentfully to his family blaming them for his impoverished state.

Just then, an auctioneer outside shouts his spiel trying to sell off his last horse. He gives the hay trusser an idea. He claims that he thinks men who don't want their wives should be allowed to sell them, too. "Why, begad, I'd sell mine this minute if somebody would buy her," he announces. The men look her over and agree that she would be worth something. If that is the case, the trusser says, he is open to an offer.

His wife begs him to stop joking but he insists that he is serious. Finally, after more rum, he makes her stand up to show herself to the crowd and calls for an auctioneer. The woman stands, remaining calm by a supreme effort of will. Someone volunteers to act as auctioneer. He'll take a guinea, the trusser says. When no one bids, he becomes incensed and gradually raises the price to five guineas. "The last time," cries the auctioneer, "Yes or no?"

"Yes," says a loud voice from the doorway where an unknown sailor stands. The hay trusser is confused. He calls for the money expecting the sailor to back out. The sailor gives it to him. Now the game is suddenly in earnest. The tension builds. Everyone becomes silent waiting to see who is bluffing.

The woman breaks in desperately, "Michael, listen to me. If you touch that money, I and the girl go with the man. Mind, it is a joke no longer." "A joke? Of course it is not a joke," Michael cries. The bargain is struck. The trusser takes the money and puts it in his pocket. His wife looks at him once, takes the baby, and begins to leave with the sailor. At the door, she turns and flings her wedding ring in his face. She is sobbing bitterly as the sailor helps her from the tent.

When she has left, Michael walks to the entrance looking out at the peaceful valley and woods. A group of horses, waiting to be taken to pasture, crosses in front of him. He staggers back into the tent, muttering that he'll not go after her. Soon, he falls into a drunken sleep on a table. The old hag leaves him there for the night.

CHAPTER II

Early the following morning, the hay trusser awakes to find himself alone in the furmity tent. As he looks around, trying to recover his wits, he comes across his wife's wedding ring on the floor. Seeing it, he vaguely begins to remember what had taken place the night before. Finding the sailor's money in his pocket proves conclusively that he has not dreamed the whole thing. He has sold his wife, Susan, and his daughter, Elizabeth-Jane, to a passing stranger.

He leaves the tent at once emerging onto the fair grounds. No one is stirring yet. He picks his way quickly through the maze of tents and booths, past the sleeping showmen and gypsies, and away from the fair. Then, he stops to reflect, leaning against a gate.

First, he wonders if he has told anyone his name; he concludes with relief that he has not. Next, he becomes angry at his wife for being such a fool and taking him so literally. He curses her simplicity of character and becomes furious at her idiotic meekness; meekness that has done him more harm than the bitterest temper, he shouts.

When he calms down, however, he realizes that he must try to find her and put up with the shame as best he can. He is a superstitious person however and, before he begins the search, he resolves to swear the greatest oath he has ever uttered; an oath so important he has to swear it in a church. He walks on. Some miles further, he comes to another village, finds the village church, and enters it. Fortunately, it is empty. Kneeling by the Communion table, he affirms loudly, "I, Michael Henchard, on this morning of the sixteenth of September, do take an oath, here in this solemn place, that I will avoid all strong liquors for the space of twenty years to come, being a year for every year that I have lived. And I swear this on the book before me; and may I be struck dumb, blind and helpless, if I break this my oath!"

Leaving the church, he sets out to trace his family. There are certain difficulties in his way, however, as he soon discovers. He doesn't even know the sailor's name and, what is worse for his search, he is too ashamed to reveal the true story to the people he questions. But he continues as best as he can. Weeks turn into months and still he searches maintaining himself by odd jobs, but he can discover no sign of them. Finally, at last, he comes to a seaport and learns that a couple and a small child answering to his description had emigrated from the port a short time before. At that, he ends his search and the next day leaves for the Southwest. He does not stop until he has reached the town of Casterbridge in a part of Wessex far away from Weydon-Priors and its fairgrounds.

Comment

The first two chapters are set apart from the remainder of the book like the prologue to a Greek tragedy. They take place almost twenty years before the main action of the novel and moreover, as in many other Hardy novels, they take place in a location far away from the central site of the book; the town of Casterbridge. Hardy does this in order to create a distance in both time and geography between the terrible act committed by Michael Henchard and what, much later, will be the consequences of that act. He purposely makes the narrative vague and dreamlike, never mentioning the characters' names until they come up in conversation, telling us nothing about their backgrounds, and so on. What he really is doing is presenting the events as Henchard would have remembered them after many years had passed.

However, Hardy indirectly tells us a great deal about the major character through his actions. He is touchy and impulsive; given to rash actions and quick judgments that he later regrets. He is ambitious and resentful of his wife and child for keeping him down and, of great importance, he is superstitious and believes strongly in the power of oaths and omens. At the same time, he is horrified and ashamed at what he has done and searches for months to find his family again.

The first two chapters also give us an idea of the primitive and almost pagan atmosphere of Wessex; its closeness to nature, its common lawlessness, and the harsh ways in which its people live. An example of Hardy's use of nature and natural things is the **irony** of the horses in Chapter One. Henchard gets the idea of selling his wife from hearing a gypsy try to auction his horse. Later, after having sold her, he looks out and sees a herd of horses being taken to pasture, and we realize that not even animals are treated in the way that Henchard has treated his wife; the horses, at least, are being cared for.

CHAPTER III

It is now exactly eighteen years after the events of the first two chapters. Again, the scene is the high road leading to Weydon-Priors and, again, two travelers can be seen walking along it. This time, however, they are both women: Sunsan Henchard and her now adult daughter, Elizabeth-Jane. The latter has become quite pretty as her mother was, but more animated, while Susan is somewhat thinner and more worn. Both of them are wearing mourning clothes.

Coming to the village, they see, or at least the mother sees, that it has changed very little since the last time they were there. A few new farm machines, a few repairs, and that is all. The fair is still being held but it has been greatly reduced in size and importance by the rise of other provincial markets.

Elizabeth-Jane wonders why they have come to this place. Her mother answers that this was the place where she first met Newson, the sailor. "First met with Father here? ... And now he's drowned and gone," laments Elizabeth-Jane.

Susan goes on to say that this was also the place where she last saw the relative they are seeking, a Mr. Michael Henchard, a "Connection by marriage". It is soon evident that Elizabeth-Jane knows nothing more about him than the little her mother has chosen to divulge.

Searching in the fair, Susan comes across an old woman "haggard, wrinkled, and almost in rags." She is selling furmity and, on close inspection, she proves to be the same old hag in whose tent the infamous sale took place. When Susan approaches her and buys a pennyworth, the hag offers to lace it with rum which evokes a bitter smile from Susan.

They converse for a while. The old hag laments the good old days when she had a booming business. Finally, Susan asks her if she remembers "the sale of a wife by a husband eighteen years ago today?"

After a moment's thought, the hag does not recall it. Only, she says, because the man happened to come back the following year and tell her in private that, if a woman ever asked for him, she was to say he had gone to - where? - she tries to remember - to Casterbridge, she thinks.

Susan thanks her and she had her daughter prepare to depart for Casterbridge.

CHAPTER IV

The history of Susan Henchard, since she had been sold by her husband, can be told in a few simple sentences. The sailor had taken Susan and her daughter to Canada where they had stayed for several years, living on the edge of poverty. When Elizabeth-Jane was twelve years old, the three had returned to England and settled in Falmouth.

As time passed, however, a change had come over Susan and she had begun to feel that it was morally wrong to live with Newson but that problem had resolved itself when Newson was lost at sea the next season. After that, all that was left in Susan's life was her daughter.

One day, shortly after the news of Newson's death, Susan had observed her daughter closely and realized that she had a great potential both for beauty and character. She had also realized than nothing would come of this potential if the two remained as poor as they were then. Elizabeth-Jane herself was constantly asking how she could become a woman of wider knowledge and higher repute - 'better' as she termed it.

Susan knew of no way to advance Elizabeth unless she swallowed her pride and went out to search for Henchard. He might well have drunk himself to death by this time, she knew, but there was no other possibility ever to make things better for her daughter. Even though they set out, however, she could not bring herself to explain who the object of their search really was. Elizabeth has remained ignorant of the true story.

From Weydon-Priors, they travel toward Casterbridge on the vague word of the furmity woman. On the journey, they are forced to live hand to mouth since they have virtually no money left and, as if that were not bad enough, it is soon clear that Susan's health is giving out. *poor*

Reaching Casterbridge on a Friday evening in September, they look down on the town from a height before entering it. "What an old-fashioned place it seems to be!" says Elizabeth-Jane. "It is all huddled together, and it is shut in by a square wall of trees, like a plot of garden-ground by a box-edging."

Before they move on, two walkers pass in heated argument. They listen and hear the name Henchard mentioned indicating that the person they seek may still be a resident of Casterbridge. They go on into the town. It is very ancient; untouched by modern times. The houses are of old brick and slate with an occasional thatched roof in sight. How the town lives is immediately obvious from the goods in its stores. Almost everything sold in them is some kind of farm implement: scythes, reap-hooks, sheep-shears, spades, hoes, carts, wheel-borrows, and the like.

Indeed. Casterbridge is so rural that it is difficult to tell where the town stops and the fields begin.

As they walk through town, curfew rings from the tower of a grizzled church. It is the signal to shut up shop and, in an instant, most of the stores on High Street have closed their shutters. As they stand there, Susan and Elizabeth hear dance music being played somewhere in the town. The sight of a woman striding past them carrying a loaf of bread reminds them that they need something to eat. They inquire of her where they can buy bread.

"There isn't any good bread in Casterbridge now," says the woman bitterly. "There's less good bread than good beer ..." Why? they ask, and the woman says that the corn-factor (the broker) has sold the millers bad wheat. She appears very angry about the sale and says that all the other poor folk are up in arms as well.

The travelers buy a substitute meal and, having nowhere to go, head instinctively toward the direction from which the music is coming.

Comment

The primary purpose of these chapters is to convey information. We are filled in on the history of Susan and Elizabeth-Jane, learn that Elizabeth-Jane does not know of Henchard, and are introduced to the town of Casterbridge. It is noteworthy that we see the town first through the eyes of Elizabeth-Jane. Hardy often uses her to comment on the appearance and activities of many people and places in the novel. When he does this, we can usually assume that she represents the author's viewpoint.

Hardy also goes out of his way to emphasize the ageless continuity and tradition of Wessex. Although eighteen years have passed, Weydon-Priors has hardly changed. The fair is still there and so is the furmity woman. Casterbridge itself is shown to be extremely old-fashioned at first glance although it is more of an urban center than Weydon-Priors.

The way we are reintroduced to Henchard is significant. Susan and Elizabeth-Jane hear two people arguing about him. He is apparently a controversial and important figure in Casterbridge. It is not difficult to put two and two together and realize that he is the corn broker about whom the woman they stop complains.

CHAPTER V

Soon they come to the spot where the town band is performing; outside the main hotel of Casterbridge. It is the King's Arms where, tonight, an important dinner is taking place. The hotel is so constructed that a large bay window opens out to the street from the main dining room. If one stands on the steps of the building across from the hotel, he can get an excellent view of the proceedings of the dinner. Some idlers are already situated on the steps when Susan and Elizabeth-Jane arrive.

Elizabeth-Jane receives permission from her mother to make inquiries about their relation. She moves up to the first step and asks an old man what is going on. He replies that she must be a stranger for sure because tonight is the night of the annual public dinner with all the leading citizens of the town. The mayor himself, Mr. Henchard, is in the chair. Susan hears the old man's words too and steps agitatedly to her daughter's side to look with her.

Through the window, directly facing them, they see a man about forty ... "Of heavy frame, large features, and commanding voice ..." He has a rich complexion which verges on swarthiness, a flashing black eye, and dark, bushy brows and hair. He seems domineering and harsh, someone to whom weakness is not to be tolerated but who is ready to admire greatness and strength. To Susan's surprise, the glasses at his place are empty except for one which contains only water.

Susan is so moved at seeing him that she shrinks back into the shadows. When Elizabeth-Jane asks if she has seen him, she replies, "Yes, yes ... It is enough for me. Now, I only want to go - pass away - die."

However, Elizabeth-Jane, very much impressed by their new-found relation, urges that they stay. Consumed with curiosity, she asks the old man at her side for more information. "Why does he not drink?" she asks. He answers that Henchard is a famous abstainer. He has sworn a gospel oath against it or so the old man has heard.

Another elderly peasant named Solomon Longways, who works for Henchard, says that the oath has two more years to run. He calls Henchard a lonely widow man. Upon being asked, he says that he only knows that he lost his wife before he came to Casterbridge. Elizabeth-Jane also discovers that Henchard is the most powerful man in town and probably the biggest grain dealer in the area. It was he who supplied the bad bread of which they had heard before.

Through the window, Henchard can be heard telling a story about how he outwitted someone in a hay deal. There is great laughing at his tale until a tradesman at the lower end of the table mutters, "This is all very well, but how about the bad bread?" The loungers outside take up the cry. The commotion becomes so great that Henchard feels he must answer it. He says he is sorry but that he lost money, too. "And the poor folk have to eat it whether or no," says someone from outside.

Henchard's face darkens and he becomes angry. He explains that these things happen in business. Since his trade has become too large for him to handle alone, he is advertising for a manager. When he gets a good one, it will not happen again.

But who will replace the bad wheat, the tradesman wants to know. "… It can't be done," answers Michael Henchard abruptly and the subject is closed.

Comment

Using a band of people who comment on the action (but do not play a major part in it) is a favorite device of Hardy's. In this case, he uses the illiterate, somewhat stupid natives as his chorus. They discuss the major character from a new viewpoint, tell the reader something about the town, and often serve to help the plot along. In addition, they provide a measure of comic relief.

The detailed description of the crowd outside the banquet room points out the almost feudal social structure of Casterbridge. The gentry are inside the hotel while the rest must stand outside and gawk. Even within the room there are social divisions. The rich landed gentry, including Henchard, sit at the head of the table and the tradesmen sit at the foot.

We get our first glimpse of Henchard through Elizabeth-Jane's eyes. She sees him as strong willed, domineering and harsh. On the other hand, she knows he must be capable and hardworking since he has risen to be mayor. The empty wine glasses also help point up his character. He swore an oath and he has kept it where most men would fail. This also shows that he must have felt some remorse for his deed.

Elizabeth-Jane's first impression of him is reinforced by his actions. She hears him telling a story about how he has defrauded someone. Everyone laughs but it is obvious that there is a great deal of resentment against him in the town. When someone mentions the bad bread, the outsiders gleefully take up the cry. Henchard's angry reaction to their needing shows that his character has changed very little since we first saw him. He still seems to be insecure and unable to stand the thought that people are opposing his will.

insecure

CHAPTER VI

Just before Henchard's last words, a young man, evidently a stranger, has come walking by. He is fair and ruddy and slight in build but with quick, bright eyes. Upon hearing Henchard say, "It can't be done," he takes out a notepad and writes a few words. "Give this to the mayor at once," he tells a waiter. Then he asks for a respectable hotel, less expensive than the King's Arms. The waiter indifferently directs him to the Three Mariners, just down the street, and he sets off. Elizabeth-Jane, who has overheard the conversation, judges from his queer accent that he must be a Scotsman.

She watches the note being handed to Henchard who seems extremely interested in its contents. While everyone around him is becoming more and more drunk, he seems preoccupied with an idea and hardly notices the others. Just then the clock strikes nine reminding Elizabeth-Jane and her mother that they must find lodgings. She remembers the Scotsman and the Three Mariners and they decide to go there.

As they leave, Henchard rises from his chair. He asks the waiter about the man who wrote the note and where he is staying. Returning to the dining room after a moment, he sees that the party is so far gone that it will not miss him and he leaves unnoticed. He strolls down the street toward the Three Mariners. He stands for a minute before the old house, observing its ancient dinginess and need for renovation. Making some adjustments on his dress, so that he will look less grand, he enters.

Comment

Here, the first important coincidence takes place. A stranger accidentally passing by suddenly becomes part of the story and immediately begins to affect it quite strongly. Susan and Elizabeth-Jane, as well as Henchard, are affected for they go to the hotel that was recommended to the young man. What is most important to notice, however, is that nothing more might come of it except that Henchard chooses to pursue the matter. This, as we will see, is true of many of the seemingly contrived coincidences in the novel. The particular events resulting from these accidents need not necessarily have taken place. Henchard always interprets and acts on the accidents in his own way. It is not they, themselves, but the way that Henchard responds to them that is important.

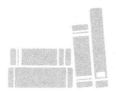

THE MAYOR OF CASTERBRIDGE

CHAPTER VII

After getting settled in their room at the Three Mariners, Susan suddenly becomes afraid that they will not be able to afford it. Elizabeth-Jane knows her mother is right but says that they must be respectable. Perhaps the landlady will let her work off some of the bill, she thinks; the custom is already out of fashion but not unheard of. The landlady, a kind woman, agrees to the suggestion. She assigns Elizabeth-Jane, as her first job, to take supper up to the Scotch gentleman.

Doing so, Elizabeth-Jane finds that his room is next to theirs up in the least expensive part of the inn and that it is equally small, also. At one time, in fact, the two rooms were probably one.

The young man hardly looks up when she enters so she has a brief chance to study him closely. She finds him quite attractive. Coming back downstairs, the landlady tells her that she had better eat her own supper now. She gives Elizabeth a tray of food for herself and her mother.

When Elizabeth-Jane brings it to their room, her mother immediately motions her to be silent. The walls are so thin that they can hear perfectly a conversation in the Scotsman's room. Susan, trembling and faint, tells Elizabeth-Jane that Henchard is the other speaker. They listen as they eat their meal.

Henchard asks if the Scot is the man who sent him the note. The Scot says yes. Henchard then says that the Scot must be the man with whom he has an appointment the next day but the Scot denies it. His name, he tell Henchard, is Donald Farfrae; it is true that he is a grain manager but he is on his way to Bristol to embark for America.

Henchard is disappointed for he thought Farfrae had come to apply for the job as his manager. He goes on to tell Farfrae that he is greatly obliged for the information in the note which, it transpires, is a new method for reclaiming bad wheat like what he had sold. He asks how much Farfrae expects to be paid if the new theory proves to be successful.

To his surprise, Farfrae demonstrates to him that the process does work and says he can have the idea for nothing. Farfrae is leaving the country for one where the invention will do him no good and he is not primarily a corn grower anyway. Henchard is greatly impressed; so much so that he offers Farfrae a job with a very good salary. The Scot regretfully refuses. Henchard then asks him at least to stay for a while at his home. Farfrae again refuses, as he must leave early the next day. Henchard is amazed that a stranger would do so much for him without asking any reward. He renews his offer, upping the wages, but Farfrae says with finality that his plans are fixed.

He offers Henchard a drink. Henchard replies that he cannot take it although he would like to. He explains that once, in drunkenness, he did a deed of which he will be ashamed until his dying day. It made such an impression on him that he swore he would drink nothing stronger than tea for twenty years. Sometimes it's been hard, he adds, but he has kept the oath.

Henchard finally leaves expressing regret once more that the young man will not stay. Farfrae says he would like to but it cannot be; he wants to see the world.

Comment

The Scot appears to be a curious person; quite different from any of the natives of Wessex. Even his name is peculiar: Farfrae. This is another of Hardy's ways of describing character. The name should be interpreted as meaning a free man who comes from far away. It is particularly important that he is free in contrast to Henchard. Henchard also comes from afar but he has never been free; neither is he free of his own character. "Character is fate."

The differences in the two men's characters becomes clearer as they talk. Henchard cannot believe that anyone would do anything freely without wanting reward. When Farfrae refuses Henchard's pressing invitation to stay, this also surprises Henchard, who cannot believe that any man would turn down a large salary.

We are also given another chance to see that Henchard is still as impulsive as ever. His emotions are always going full force. When he approves of something, he is overwhelming in his friendship. If he decides he has no use for it, he will cast it aside without thinking twice. *bi polav*

CHAPTER VIII

After Henchard leaves, Farfrae rings the bell to have his supper removed and goes downstairs to the bar. Elizabeth-Jane gets his tray and follows him down the stairs. Farfrae has just joined the regulars in the general sitting room when she comes down. She pauses and watches the scene from near the door.

The Scot soon makes himself at home. Someone asks him to favor him with a song. He complies with a beautiful Scotch **ballad** about his "ain countree". He sings so well and with such emotion that the room becomes hushed. There is great applause when he has finished and they urge him to sing another, remarking that people in this part of the country never feel that strongly about where they live. "Danged if our country down here is worth singing about like that," they agree.

Christopher Coney, the old man with whom Elizabeth-Jane had talked earlier, jokingly says the people around Casterbridge aren't honest enough to be sung about. Farfrae, typically, takes him seriously and says it can't be true. The rest tell him it was not seriously meant and ask for another song. By this time, he has completely won over the affections of the people in the bar. Even the landlady, who almost never shifts her huge weight from her chair by the cashbox, has turned and moved over to hear better. She asks him if he is staying in Casterbridge. No, he answers, he is only passing through.

"We be truly sorry to hear it," says Solomon Longways. He comments how unusual it is to meet a man who comes from the land of perpetual snow; "where wolves and wild boars and other dangerous animalcules (sic) be as common as blackbirds hereabout." Farfrae tells him, at first sadly, that the man is mistaken. There are no wolves and not that much snow and, he adds enthusiastically: "But you should take a summer jarreny to Edinboro' ... and Arthur's seat ... and the lochs ... and you would never say 'tis land of wolves and perpetual snow."

Are you taking much with you, Coney asks. Farfrae replies that he has already sent his few belongings on ahead. He adds, "... Never a one of the prizes of life will I come by unless I undertake it! And I decided to go."

The entire company gives a regretful sigh. Elizabeth-Jane, in particular, is sorry for she immediately feels that she has much in common with the Scot. He is serious and melancholy, like herself, and unlike the others in Casterbridge.

Farfrae decides to retire early. The landlady hurriedly sends Elizabeth-Jane to turn down his bed. She meets Farfrae just as she is leaving his room. They pause and Farfrae smiles at her making her blush.

When she returns to her mother, she finds Susan worried about something new. Susan says that she should not, under any circumstances, have worked for their supper. This is because, if Henchard does decide to help them and learns where they had stayed and what Elizabeth-Jane had done, it would affront his pride as mayor. Elizabeth-Jane claims that he shouldn't mind because the person she had served was so much better than the rest of the guests.

Comment

As in chapter five, a group of local rustics is used to illustrate a point about the major characters and tells us facts about the area. They show us at once how different Farfrae is from

BRIGHT NOTES STUDY GUIDE

the people of Wessex; they comment on it themselves. He is much more serious than the local people; he is much more sentimental about such things as country and home. On the other hand, except for his songs, he has little of their sense of humor of lightness.

Elizabeth-Jane begins to fall in love with him when she hears him sing and we are led to feel that the two of them would make a good pair.

The ease with which Farfrae gets along with the illiterate and unintelligent natives is also remarkable and contrasts greatly with Henchard's attitude toward them. Henchard felt that he had to tone down his appearance; to lower himself before entering the inn.

Susan reinforces the idea the Henchard is acutely conscious of social distinctions by her fear of his anger over Elizabeth-Jane's employment. And Susan, we gradually realize, usually knows what she is about when speaking of her husband.

CHAPTER IX

The next morning Elizabeth-Jane rises early. She throws open the shutters and looks out. Almost immediately, she ducks back into the room for she sees that the Scot in the next room has done the same thing. He is leaning out of his window, speaking to Henchard, who happened to be walking past just then.

Henchard asks if he is off soon. Farfrae says yes, he is; it is such a fine morning that he thinks he will walk a bit and let the coach pick him up on the way. Henchard invites him to walk along with him. They will both be going in the same direction, out the Bristol road ... for a while anyway.

Elizabeth-Jane watches as they leave, talking animatedly, until they are out of sight. Although she knows it is silly, she is somewhat put out by the fact that Farfrae had glanced at her in the window as he left but did not say goodbye.

Susan finally decides this morning that she should let Henchard know they are in Casterbridge. Since he has been so friendly to the Scot, a stranger, perhaps he will be the same with them. She sends a message with Elizabeth-Jane, who is to say that Henchard's relative Susan, a sailor's widow, is in town; she would leave it to him whether he would recognize her. "If he says no," Susan tells her daughter, "say, 'then sir, we would rather not intrude; we will leave Casterbridge as quietly as we have come, and go back to our own country.'"

"And tell him," Susan continues, "that I fully know I have no claim upon him; that I am glad to find he is thriving; that I hope his life may be long and happy."

Elizabeth-Jane sets out up the High Street. It is market day and she is in no hurry. She strolls past the private houses of the gentry, observing the old-fashioned bow windows and the flower gardens. Since it is market day, tradesmen and farmers from all over the country have come to buy and sell their produce. Vans are set up everywhere. Goods have been propped up for display halfway out into the street. Horses for sale are tied in long rows and, in front of them, pigs and geese. One can easily see that Casterbridge was as much a part of the country as any farm. There is no other business but agriculture.

Passing through the market, it is not long before Elizabeth-Jane comes to Henchard's house. It is one of the best and largest in town with spacious grounds; as one would expect of the mayor. She asks for Henchard and is taken to the granary yard. He does not come, however, and finally she asks someone else who directs her to the office. To her great astonishment, however, it is not Henchard but Farfrae whom she finds there. He asks her to wait as Henchard will be back in a minute. He has not recognized her.

How Farfrae came to be there is easily explained. He and Henchard, on their walk that morning, had stopped at the highest point in Casterbridge to say goodbye. They had looked out at the beautiful view of the countryside, its fertile farms and neat fields and woods. Henchard had once more offered him the job. This time, however, the Scot, gazing out at the countryside in the full bloom of autumn, had begun to waver. An instant later, he had declared, "It's providence! Should anyone go against it? No, I'll not go to America; I'll stay and be your man!"

"Done," had said Henchard as they shook hands. He had given Farfrae his breakfast and taken him around his establishment and had finally installed him in the offices where Elizabeth-Jane has just found him.

CHAPTER X

As Elizabeth-Jane sits waiting for Henchard, a man enters the office. He jumps in front of her when Henchard arrives and introduces himself.

"Joshua Jopp, sir - by appointment - the new manager!" he says. Henchard tells him it is too late; he has already engaged someone else. The man protests; Henchard replies that he was to have come on Thursday. Thursday or Saturday, Jopp cries, and shows Henchard's letter to prove his point. "You as good as engaged me," he says. Henchard harshly repeats that he is too late and Jopp storms out.

Elizabeth-Jane now enters his office and delivers her message. Henchard is stunned. Recovering with difficulty, he asks her what name she goes by. "Elizabeth-Jane Newson," she answers. From this Henchard guesses that his daughter knows nothing of the true story. His wife has been kinder to him that he had a right to expect.

Taking her into his house, he gradually draws the full story from Elizabeth-Jane. Even when he talks to her, however, he cannot keep his voice from trembling. Noticing her shabby clothes, he inquires whether her "father" has left them much money. Elizabeth says no. At once Henchard takes out a five pound note and puts it in an envelope. He also includes a short letter to Susan. At the last second, he thoughtfully adds five more shillings, bringing the amount to exactly what he had received from Newson many years before. When she rises to return to her mother, he watches her leave with strong but very mixed emotions.

Elizabeth-Jane gives the letter to her mother. It reads: "Meet me at eight o'clock this evening, if you can, at Ring on the Budmouth road. The place is easy to find. I can say no more now. This news upsets me almost. The girl seems to be in ignorance. Keep her so till I have seen you. M.H."

Comment

In chapters nine and ten, we see again how Henchard acts when he is really determined. It is not accident that he is walking by the inn in the morning and invites Farfrae to walk with him. Indeed, he almost seems to have a compulsive attraction toward the Scot which will have bittter consequences later. The point is made quite emphatically that Henchard is the one who sows the seeds of his own destruction by convincing Farfrae to remain.

We see Henchard dealing with three very different people. Each meeting represents a facet of his character. Talking to Farfrae, he is energetic and bustling. With Jopp he is ruthless; not evincing the slightest consideration. With Elizabeth-Jane he is gentle and kind and appears genuinely moved by finding his family again. However, the manner in which he contacts his wife is revealing. He does not go directly to her because he fears it will jeopardize his standing in the town. He shows his true feelings toward Susan when he symbolically offers to buy her back by enclosing five guineas in the note. It is a gesture that appeals to Henchard almost as a business transaction. The tone of his note hints that, while he knows his duty, he is not especially happy about having to perform it.

CHAPTER XI

The Ring at Casterbridge was the name of an old, crumbling Roman amphitheater; one of the finest remaining in Britain. Indeed, Casterbridge itself (and the area around it) was one of the oldest historically interesting places in the country. It had been an important Roman town over 1500 years before. Even at the time, it was still common to dig up a skeleton of a Roman when working in the fields and Roman artifacts were an everyday thing. The Ring itself was a vast sinister ruin where local people often met for secret purposes ... usually of an illegal nature. Rarely, however, did lovers go there. There was something about the place that frightened them; something derived from the spirit of the witch burnings and gladiatorial contests for which it had been used in the past. It was, however, the most secluded location in town which is why Henchard had chosen it for the meeting place.

Henchard arrives early. Susan comes just after the assigned time. They meet in the center of the arena and, for a moment, neither speaks as he supports her in his arms.

"I don't drink," are his first words. "You hear, Susan? - I don't drink now - I haven't since that night." He goes on to say that he had assumed she was dead by now and wants to know why she has kept silent all this time. She answers that she had felt herself bound to Newson. She comes now only as Newson's widow and she does not feel that she has a claim on Henchard. They speak of their daughter and agree that she must be kept in ignorance. Henchard also points out that, even though he would like to bring them into his home at once, his position in the town makes that impossible; there would be too many questions.

Susan offers to leave. He laughs at her simplicity. He has a plan, he says, which will solve the problem. It is that she and Elizabeth-Jane take up residence in the town and he will court her and marry her again. That way, no one will hear of his disgraceful youth and the result will be just the same. Officially, Elizabeth-Jane will become his stepdaughter.

Susan agrees meekly saying she will leave everything in his hands. As they part, Henchard asks, "Do you forgive me, Susan?"

She murmurs something indistinguishable. "Never mind - all in good time," he says. "Judge me by my future works - goodbye!"

Comment

As he did in chapter four, Hardy makes use of the forbidding atmosphere of Casterbridge to present the mood of his story. Henchard and Susan meet in a gloomy, ancient, memory-ridden ruin; symbolic of their marriage. Henchard goes on with his pretense that they can begin everything again. He has already given back the sale money symbolically and his new plan will have them remarry. In this way, he is pretending to his conscience that he has wiped the slate clean. It is noteworthy, however, that Hardy makes a point of telling us that true lovers do not go to the Ring. Susan too seems to feel that everything is not as simple as Henchard would like to have it. And the very fact that Henchard insists so strongly that he has changed, indicates that he is not quite convinced that he can quiet his conscience by starting again at this late date.

CHAPTER XII

Back at his own house, Henchard notices that Donald Farfrae is still working over the books in the office. He goes in and watches the Scot without interrupting him. Farfrae is trying to restore order to the ledgers which have become almost unreadable due to Henchard's inability to keep clear figures. Henchard is unfit by character to grub around in account books which is why, he reflects, he wanted a manager in the first place. Watching Farfrae, he admires his dexterity with the books. At the same time, he feels a slight pity for anyone who is willing to give his mind to such minute details.

Henchard insists that Farfrae stop after a while. Bringing him into the house, he gives him dinner despite Farfrae's desire to return home. They eat and then settle before the fire for a talk. Henchard tells his manager he is a lonely man, with no one to talk to, and wants to tell Farfrae about a family matter. Farfrae says he will be glad to listen if he can be of any service.

Henchard then tells him the entire story of his relations with Susan and his daughter. Farfrae advises him to take Susan back and live with her and try to make amends. Henchard answers that is what he intends to do but that there is a complication. "By doing right with Susan, I wrong another innocent woman," he says.

He goes on to relate that for many years he has been accustomed to going to Jersey on business during the potato and root season. Once, however, after he had gone there, he became extremely sick and at the same time very depressed in a violent way that Farfrae has never experienced. A young woman there took pity on him and nursed him back to health. They became intimate and their relations caused a scandal. It made little difference to him but it ruined her reputation. She suffered a great deal after he left, and did not neglect to remind him of it in letter after letter. Finally, Henchard felt he could be sure that Susan was dead and he offered to make amends to the girl by marrying her. She had joyfully accepted.

But now Susan has arrived and he must disappoint the second girl and make her suffer even more. Farfrae advised him to write to the girl and tell her the truth. "That won't do," replies Henchard, "I shall have to send her money as well." He asks Farfrae to draft the letter since he is no good with words. Farfrae consents to do so.

Finally, Henchard asks him what he feels he should do about Elizabeth-Jane. Farfrae suggests admitting the truth to her and she'll forgive him. "Never!" replies Henchard; he would lose her respect immediately. At that, the conversation ends. Farfrae makes up a letter and Henchard copies and posts it, hoping that it will be enough to resolve the problem.

Comment

Henchard continues to act in a way which distinguishes him from everyone else in the novel. Farfrae, we see, is orderly and painstaking; a neat person. Henchard is the opposite; a grander, more expansive figure but also less prudent. This is shown by the necessity of having Farfrae edit his books and correct the mistakes in them. That relationship also seems to be carrying over into their private lives. Henchard asks Farfrae to edit his life for him by telling Farfrae the story of his marriage. Farfrae gives sound advice for someone else but not for Henchard. He is basically unable to understand his employer just as he has never experienced the kind of violent depression which led to Henchard's affair in Jersey. Farfrae has the proper sentiments but he is somewhat shallow. The tormented depths of Henchard's character are beyond him.

CHAPTER XIII

Henchard finds a cottage in the western part of town and there he puts Susan and Elizabeth-Jane. They go, of course, under the name of Newson. Immediately after they are settled, Henchard begins to pay them a great many visits. He comes to tea often and he and Susan go to great pains to hoodwink their daughter. Henchard seems to take a grim pleasure in this deception. Susan is less pleased but she has no choice. One day Henchard says drily, when Elizabeth is out, "This is a very good opportunity for me to ask you to name the happy day, Susan." She protests that he is wasting his time on her but he is determined to make up for the way he has treated her. They set a day in the near future.

Henchard's obvious courting of the widow causes much comment in the town. No one can understand why Henchard, an avowed woman-hater, has suddenly decided to marry Mrs. Newson. As a joke, people in the town refer to her as "The Ghost" because she is so thin and pale. The mayor presses on relentlessly however.

The wedding day arrives. A carriage comes to get Susan and Elizabeth-Jane. It is the first time either of them has ever ridden in one. Susan and Henchard are married at the town church with Donald Farfrae acting as best man. Outside the church, the town idlers have gathered to discuss the event. They joke about the bride and tease Mother Cuxsom, the fat lady from the Three Mariners. "How's this?" says Solomon Longways, "Here's Mrs. Newson, a mere skellington, has got another husband to keep her, while a woman of your tonnage have not."

They talk about the old days, and the times they used to have, until the wedding couple emerges. Some of the spectators predict a hard life for the new Mrs. Henchard. There's a bluebeardy look about the mayor, they claim. Others disagree; they feel there isn't a better catch in the whole country. The pair drive off and the rest go to have a drink.

Comment

In so obviously courting Susan, Henchard makes himself an object of unflattering discussion to the town. The loafers comment on it as probably do the gentry as well. Knowing Henchard's dislike of his social inferiors and how he hates to be made a fool of, we know that a deep compulsion must be driving him to go on with the plan despite the derision it encounters. It is another indication of his deep guilt that he perseveres. There is even a hint that he subconsciously wants to make himself suffer for his misdeed.

CHAPTER XIV

With the move into Henchard's house, Elizabeth-Jane enters into a new period in her life. For the first time, she has everything she needs. And, even more, she finds that if she wants something else all she must do is ask for it and it is hers. Henchard will grant her every wish. As a consequence, the potential which her mother had seen in her begins to develop. Physically, she becomes very attractive. The lines on her face go away, her figure fills out, and her complexion improves with good food and care. At the same time, however, she does not change much in character. She remains serious and thoughtful most of the time. Like most people who have been poor, she somehow feels that, if she lets herself be too happy, it all might disappear. "I wouldn't be too gay on any account," she says to herself. "It would be tempting Providence to hurl mother and me down and afflict us again as He used to."

Henchard is very fond of her. Occasionally, he almost lets it slip out that he knew her when she was a baby. After one of those slips, which Elizabeth-Jane fortunately fails to notice, he tells

Susan that he wants his daughter to go by her real name ... not as Miss Newson. Susan protests but he insists. He says he will advertise it in the paper if the girl agrees. Susan discusses it with her, but Elizabeth-Jane indicates to Henchard that she would not be happy about the change. He abruptly drops the request.

Meanwhile, Henchard's business prospers as never before under the direction of Donald Farfrae. Elizabeth-Jane, from her bedroom window, often watches the two of them working. She notices the fierce affection Henchard has for Farfrae; almost as if he were his son. She notices too that Farfrae often observes her and her mother with curiosity. She does not know, of course, that this is because Farfrae knows the true story of their presence.

One day she receives a message, by hand, that she should meet the writer (who does not give his name) in a section of Casterbridge called Durnover. Since her stepfather has a granary there, she assumes it is a matter of business. Upon going there, however, she finds it empty. Soon Donald Farfrae enters. Suddenly overcome by shyness, and not wanting to meet him alone, she hides inside the granary. Farfrae also seems to be waiting for someone. She makes an accidental noise; he sees her and enters the granary. The two soon discover that both had received identical notes asking them to meet someone there. They decide to wait for whomever it was. When it begins to rain, they move farther inside for shelter. No one comes. Farfrae says it must have been a trick. Neither of them is in a hurry to leave, however. Elizabeth-Jane says Farfrae must be anxious to return to Scotland, judging from the song he sang. He says no; it was just a song. After a bit more chatting, she says she must go. Farfrae points out that she is covered with wheat husks and helps her brush them off. He watches her go thoughtfully.

THE MAYOR OF CASTERBRIDGE

CHAPTERS 15–24

CHAPTER XV

Because Elizabeth-Jane dresses conservatively and keeps to herself, few people in the town notice how pretty she is becoming. One day, Henchard gives her a bright pair of gloves. She wants to wear them to please him but she has to buy a bonnet to go with them; then, of course, she needs a dress ... and then a sunshade. The first time that she wears them, the town discovers her. She becomes so popular that her good fortune frightens her. She tells herself she doesn't deserve to be admired because she is uneducated and almost convinces herself to sell her finery and buy books instead.

Another day, she is watching Henchard and Farfrae from her window. It is about six o'clock and the men are going home. As the last one is leaving, Henchard calls to him. He warns him that, if he is not on time the next day, there will be trouble. Then he lets him go. The worker he has warned is named Abel Whittle. He is second hand at the hay-weighing ... an important job. Twice that week he had been late thus holding up the rest for almost an hour each time.

The next day he is late again. Henchard, true to his word, rushes to his house and pulls him out of bed. Refusing to let him pause to put on his breeches, he hauls him off to the yard like a naughty child. Farfrae sees him there and asks him what on earth is going on. Whittle explains. He says he will kill himself from embarrassment at the end of the day. Farfrae tells him to go home and get dressed like a man. Henchard walks up and demands, "Who's sending him back?" Farfrae says he is. Henchard says the man stays. A contest of wills develops, neither backs down. "Come," says Farfrae, "A man in your position should ken better, sir!" Henchard gives in sullenly muttering that Farfrae is taking advantage of him because he was fool enough to tell him the secret of his life. "I had forgot it," answers Farfrae.

In the next days, Henchard begins to resent the Scot violently. One morning a boy comes to fetch Farfrae to value a load of hay and Henchard says he will go. The boy says they want Farfrae. Henchard questions the boy and learns that Farfrae is much more highly thought of than he; both as a business man and as a person. People say they wish he was the master instead of Henchard, the boy informs him. Henchard goes anyway. On the way he meets Farfrae. During their conversation, Henchard accuses him of being careful of everyone's feelings except his. Farfrae apologizes if he has done anything. He says he didn't mean to. Henchard accepts his statement and immediately feels better. The two of them part with renewed friendship.

Comment

Once again, we see the action through the eyes of Elizabeth-Jane. Hardy uses her, as he did to describe the town of Casterbridge, as a kind of objective, outside commentator on the action. She expresses an important cornerstone of his philosophy; that no one can ever be sure of happiness, no matter how well things may be going at any moment. This truth applies to all of the major figures in the novel but particularly to Henchard.

These two chapters mark the beginning of Henchard's decline. For the first time he is balked in his desires: first by Elizabeth-Jane, who refuses his name, and then by Farfrae in the matter of Abel Whittle. It is typical of Hardy's method that these two events are more than just indicators of Henchard's character. They will later become important turning points in the plot as well.

Henchard's compulsion to dominate and acquire everything close to him comes out in both of these incidents. The **episode** with Elizabeth-Jane is particularly significant. He tries to acquire her like a piece of property just as he had "repurchased" his wife. He fails to realize that human relationships are more than legal or business transactions.

CHAPTER XVI

Despite having resolved their differences, Henchard remains suspicious of Farfrae. He becomes much more reserved toward him and treats him more like a business associate than a close friend.

Things continue in this way until, one day, Farfrae asks if Henchard would mind lending him some rick-cloths. Farfrae wants to use them to get up an entertainment to celebrate a recent national event. Henchard gives him the cloths but immediately becomes jealous. He feels that it is his place as mayor to initiate such occasions.

Consequently, Henchard sets about to create a really brilliant social affair. He intends to hold it on the same day as Farfrae's and show him up. Henchard's will be larger, more impressive, and, what is more, it will be free. Choosing the best location in the area, he builds a huge party site complete with hurdles, rings, poles, and so on for games, prepares a great amount of food and drink and all the rest. He also prints posters and puts them up all over town. Occasionally, he walks by Farfrae's preparations, sneering at their insignificance.

The party day arrives. About noon it begins to storm. Henchard has made no provision for bad weather and his party is ruined. Only a few brave souls appear. The tables, the games, the food, and everything else are practically swept away by the torrent of rain.

The rain finally stops but still no one comes. He asks someone where they are. At Farfrae's, he is told. Later, he morosely goes for a walk and notices that everyone seems to be headed for a particular part of town. Following them, he is led to Farfrae's entertainment. To his chagrin, he sees the Scot has chosen a spot where the trees are quite dense. He has covered some of the closest with a canvas, making a kind of pavilion to protect against the rain. Henchard goes in. He finds a ball in progress; an altogether new idea for Casterbridge. Farfrae himself is the main attraction. He dances like a madman. Henchard can see from the women's faces that he is greatly admired. Even Elizabeth-Jane is there and dances with Farfrae.

Henchard also hears people saying how lucky he is that Farfrae came along and saved his business. Some even approach him and tease him about Farfrae. They say that Farfrae, having taken the weather into consideration, is a perfect example of better sense. Henchard becomes angry. He announces that Farfrae will not be working for him much longer. He leaves in a jealous fit.

CHAPTER XVII

Elizabeth-Jane leaves the pavilion conscious that she has done something to offend her stepfather. She thinks he is angry because she had lowered herself by dancing in the common crowd. Walking alone, she is joined by Farfrae. He says he had hoped to have another dance with her. He tells her he no longer works for her father and may soon be leaving Casterbridge. Both of them are unhappy over his words. Nervously, Farfrae says that, if he was richer, he would ask her something in a short time. "Yes," he says, "I would ask you tonight; but that's not for me!" Elizabeth-Jane admits she hopes he stays and they part.

She thinks of him a great deal in the next days. When she learns that he has purchased a small feed business in opposition to her father, she is alternately glad and unhappy. Henchard, on the other hand, is violently angry. He forbids her to see Farfrae and sends him a note informing him of this. He also resolves to crush Farfrae in business.

However, Farfrae's trade grows. Even though he refuses to compete for Henchard's customers, there are plenty to go around. At first, he tries to ignore Henchard's attacks on him but he soon realizes it is a matter of survival for him. They begin to fight commercially but, for all Henchard's efforts, the Scot's business continues to grow.

Comment

The struggle between Henchard and Farfrae begins in earnest. As always, however, it need not have. It is Henchard who causes his own humiliation by setting up a competing entertainment. It is Henchard who dispenses with the services of Farfrae. When Farfrae sets up as an independent grain dealer, it is Henchard who tries to drive him out of business, thus ensuring his own destruction. During all of these antagonisms, the Scot's actions are always defensive.

These two chapters also mark the high point of Farfrae's and Elizabeth-Jane's relations. In a sense, it is prophetic when Farfrae says she is not for him; at least not in the near future.

CHAPTER XVIII

Susan's health, poor at best, finally begins to give out. During her illness, Henchard receives a letter from Jersey. In it, the other girl, whose name is Lucetta, says she understands his decision and approves of it; there was nothing else he could have done, she agrees. She thanks him for the money and asks only one thing more: that he return all her letters. She says she will be passing through Casterbridge in the near future and he can meet her briefly and give them over. Henchard, though wary, decides he must do as she asks.

Meanwhile, Susan is dying. She tries to conclude her affairs before she goes. First, she writes a letter, seals it, and locks it in her desk. It is addressed "Mr. Michael Henchard ... not to be opened till Elizabeth-Jane's wedding day." Later, Susan tells her daughter that it was she who had sent the notes to her and Donald Farfrae that day. It was because she wanted them to fall in love all marry. But now, they agree unhappily, there is little chance of that. In a few days, Susan is dead.

Comment

The first part of the novel ends and the second begins. The old epoch concludes with the death of Susan and the revelation in the next chapter of Elizabeth-Jane's true father.

On the surface, Susan's death and Lucetta's entrance into the story are highly coincidental. Actually, their conjunction is symbolic. With the exit of one woman from the guilty past, another arrives to take her place. She brings with her additional problems and additional misdeeds for Henchard to redress.

The name Lucetta, like Farfrae, is revealing. It is a foreign name, unEnglish, indicating that she is different from the Wessex natives. It is romantic and sensual; far from the commonplace Susans and Elizabeths.

CHAPTER XIX

Three weeks later, Henchard and Elizabeth-Jane are sitting before the fire conversing. Henchard asks her if she remembers much about her early youth and whether her father was a good man. She calls Newson a good man. In his loneliness, Henchard tells her that she is his daughter although he conceals the circumstances by which Newson met her mother. He asks her again to change her name to his. He pleads with her to accept him as her real father and to love him. In a kind of daze, she agrees to the change. Henchard then leaves her to her thoughts with the promise that tomorrow he will show her some documents to prove his statements.

He goes upstairs and opens his desk. Among his papers, he finds the letter Susan had written before she died along with her few other records. The seal has already come off. Henchard thinks nothing of opening it using this as an excuse. It reads, "...I have kept one thing a secret from you till now.... Elizabeth-Jane is not your Elizabeth-Jane; the child who was in my arms when you sold me. No; she died three months after that and this living one is my other husband's...."

The information is a terrible blow to Henchard. He doesn't know what to believe. Going to Elizabeth-Jane's bedroom, where she is sleeping, he gazes in at her. He sees, to his horror, that she does resemble Newson and not him. He is forced to accept the opinion that Susan was telling the truth. He rushes from the house walking down by the river. Everything is still and gloomy. He comes to the town gallows. It looks incomplete without a corpse dangling from it. He shudders. It seems to symbolize the frustration of his ambitions. He returns to the house bitter and disappointed.

Elizabeth-Jane is very cheerful the next day. She tells Henchard that she is happy he is her real father. Newson was kind but, "That's not the same thing as being one's real father, after all."

Henchard is unable to deny it. He resolves to keep up the pretense despite the ruination of all his dreams.

Comment

The letter that Susan wrote before her death provides the link between the first two parts of the novel. By informing Henchard of Elizabeth-Jane's true ancestry, she cuts him off completely from the distant past. There is no one left to whom he owes anything or, at least, no family. At the same time, the letter triggers the events which lead to Elizabeth-Jane's change of address and all that the change causes. We see Henchard cannot escape from his guilt. Circumstances and his character still work hand in hand to frustrate him. If Susan had not written the letter, the ensuing event would not have occurred. On the other hand, another man might have followed her instructions and not opened it.

CHAPTER XX

To Elizabeth-Jane's distress, Henchard becomes increasingly cold and critical of her. He complains about her grammar and her use of dialect slang. He invariably seems to find something amiss with her. Whenever they meet, usually at mealtime, the girl studies and tries to improve but nothing she does satisfies him. There is an incident over her handwriting. Henchard asks her to copy out an agreement for him but tears it up because her handwriting is not ladylike enough. Finally, his antagonism reaches a **climax** when he chastises her for bringing a drink to Nance Mockridge, an old peasant woman who works in the yards. He insults Nance by telling Elizabeth-Jane she is lowering herself by serving her. Nance retaliates by informing him that Elizabeth-Jane once worked as a serving girl at the Three Mariners. Henchard is humiliated. He feels that his reputation has been destroyed. From that time, he hardly speaks to Elizabeth-Jane.

She is extremely unhappy; she sees no one. Even Farfrae has not spoken to her since he received Henchard's note. One day that winter, as is her habit, she goes to visit Susan's grave. There is someone there before her, however. If is a young woman, expensively dressed, whom Elizabeth-Jane has never seen before. She cannot held admiring her beauty and grace. It is immediately apparent that this is someone of far greater sophistication than is the rule in Casterbridge. The stranger stands before Susan's grave a long time and then leaves the cemetery.

Elizabeth-Jane has another scene with Henchard when she returns. This one is so bad that Henchard declares, "I'm burned, if it goes on, this house can't hold us two." With that thought in mind, he writes to Farfrae telling him he has no objection to his courting his daughter, as long as Farfrae doesn't come in the house. Henchard hopes now to marry her off and be done with it.

The next day, Elizabeth-Jane goes again to the churchyard. Farfrae passes her on the way but he ignores her. Depressed by the fact that she is completely unwanted, she sits tearfully and thinks about her position. Without realizing she is speaking out loud, she says, "Oh, I wish I was dead with dear mother!"

Suddenly, she looks up to find the young woman she had noticed before sitting beside her. The woman asks what the matter is. She inquires about Mr. Henchard, and seems to know something about him. Eventually, Elizabeth-Jane tells her the whole story of her history. She asks the woman what she can do for she must do something. The woman asks her if she would like to come live with her and be her companion. Elizabeth-Jane demurs. She says she has no social accomplishments. The woman says that doesn't matter; she intends to set up house in

Casterbridge in a house called High Place Hall and she would like her to live there. Elizabeth-Jane joyfully assents.

CHAPTER XXI

Elizabeth-Jane goes into town where she hears a good deal of curiosity being expressed in the shops about the new tenant. She decides to have a look at High Place Hall. It is quite an imposing structure, built like an old 18th century mansion. It is the only one of its kind in the town. In fact, its massive grey stone facade and parapet look directly out over the market. For the last two years it has been vacant because of that view. It was generally felt by the gentry that to have a marketplace just under one's nose was unbecoming. Therefore, those who could have afforded it chose to live somewhere else.

Elizabeth-Jane impulsively enters through the front door. She becomes frightened, however, and quickly leaves by another exit. To her surprise, she finds herself in a dark old alley which must have been used as a secret entrance years ago. Few people in the town today know of its existence. A broken gargoyle over the arch leers at her and makes her uneasy. Just then she hears footsteps and hides herself. She does not dare look out. Had she done so, she would have seen that the person coming up the alley is none other than Henchard. When the newcomer has passed, she hurries home.

That night, she asks Henchard if he minds if she leaves his home. She says she has an offer of a position. He appears absolutely indifferent. He has no objections and even offers to give her a small annuity. She accepts.

She has a meeting with the young woman who introduces herself as Miss Templeman. They decide that Elizabeth-Jane should move in right away. Miss Templeman says that, since Henchard has given his consent without knowing where it is Elizabeth-Jane is going, perhaps they had better not say until she has actually left.

Elizabeth-Jane goes home to pack. Henchard sees her. He is taken aback at how quickly she is leaving. He says he thought she had meant sometime in the future. She takes her things to a carriage outside. Henchard suddenly has a change of heart. He asks her to remain. Elizabeth-Jane, as politely as she can, refuses. Henchard nods. "Where is she going?" he asks. She tells him. When he hears the words "High Place Hall" he freezes in astonishment. Elizabeth-Jane waves gaily to him as she drives off.

Comment

We see in the last two chapters how swiftly Henchard has ceased to be the leader and master of events. In the first part of the novel, his word was law. Now his wishes are ignored and plots are formulated and successfully carried out behind his back. The process of stripping him gradually of all his possessions is beginning Elizabeth-Jane is only the first of these to go. When he finally does realize that he has driven her away, it is too late to stop it. This will be the pattern throughout the remainder of the novel. Henchard comes to understand; but, always, too late.

Lucetta's first appearance is significant. We see her in the cemetery symbolically taking Susan's place as Elizabeth-Jane's companion. It is also apparent, both from her appearance and the ease with which she handles Elizabeth-Jane, that she will be a much more formidable person for Henchard to deal with than was Susan.

CHAPTER XXII

The night before, Henchard had received a letter from Lucetta. In it, she said that she was now living at High Place Hall. She has come to Casterbridge, she claims, because she had heard of the death of Mrs. Henchard. She hints that they are now free to marry and she has come to offer Henchard the opportunity, if he wants it. In a postscript, she says something surprising has happened about which she will tell him when he comes.

Henchard had gone that night through the back alley. He had asked for Miss LeSueur, Lucetta's real surname, and been told that only Miss Templeman was in. Assuming Lucetta was not at home, he had left.

The next day, he receives another note from Lucetta. She tells him she has taken the name of Templeman; that of an aunt of hers who has recently died and left her some property. She goes on to say that the reason she has encouraged Elizabeth-Jane to move in with her is to give Henchard a reason for visiting.

Henchard is pleased. Although he is no longer much in love with her, he is lonely. He decides that he will marry her. That night, he goes to High Place Hall but she is not expecting him so soon and is too busy to see him. She has the servant say she hopes he will come the next day. To teach her a lesson, however, he resolves he will make her wait awhile.

On Elizabeth-Jane's arrival, she is shown into the parlor where Lucetta waits. Looking at her closely, Elizabeth-Jane sees that Lucetta is a few years older than she. They talk and the girl is greatly impressed by Lucetta's poise and sophistication. Lucetta tells her that she is from Jersey where she spoke both French and English as a child. Elizabeth-Jane is envious. She can't even learn Latin, she says, while Lucetta speaks both French and Italian fluently.

The next morning Lucetta awaits Henchard. He does not come. This happens for several days and she becomes worried. Although she is no longer passionately in love with him, any more than he is with her, she too feels that it would be good for them to get married. After talking with Elizabeth-Jane, she decides that Henchard is staying away because he dislikes his daughter. Hence, Lucetta's clever scheme has turned into a disaster. She abruptly gets rid of Elizabeth-Jane for the day and writes to Henchard that he can come now. Telling her servant to admit a gentleman caller as soon as he rings, she sits down to wait. She hears the servant showing someone i. Flinging the door open, she greets him nervously; but the man before her is not Henchard.

Comment

For the first time, the two headstrong, proud personalities of the novel come into direct conflict. Neither's character will allow the other to become dominant. They lay traps for each other hoping to achieve some kind of superiority. Lucetta is shown to be very much like Henchard. She, too, must always have her way and she, too, is not above using other people to gain it. Both of them act in a very similar manner toward Elizabeth-Jane. When they have a reason for wanting her around, they are as nice as could be. As soon as it appears that she can no longer be of use, they abruptly get rid of her.

CHAPTER XXIII

"Oh," cries Lucetta. "I've made a mistake!"

Farfrae, a little bewildered, apologizes for having come in upon her like this. He says he had asked for Miss Henchard, and was shown up to Lucetta. He asks if this is the right house. To ease his embarrassment, Lucetta invites him to sit down for a while. She, like Elizabeth-Jane, finds him somewhat attractive.

They talk about the market outside. At first, both of them are uneasy but soon Lucetta regains her poise. She mentions that she is alone and knows no one in Casterbridge; like him, she comes from far away. Farfrae points out, through the window, a person in the market. He tells a story about how he outsmarted the man in business. He becomes so excited by his story that he ends by forgetting himself and slamming his fist down on the tea table for emphasis.

Lucetta becomes more interested. She embarrasses him by comparing her character to his as a Scot. Again, looking out at the market, they see and hear an unhappy transaction take place. A young man and his aged father are negotiating with another farmer to go to work for the latter. The farmer insists that he will take both or neither which means that the son must leave his sweetheart and go with his father. She is crying. Both Lucetta and Farfrae are upset by the scene. Farfrae decides that he will hire them since he needs someone anyway; thus solving the problem. He leaves, speaks to them, settles the matter, and returns.

A little later they see another farmer looking for someone. Farfrae remembers that he had an appointment with him.

He wants to stay but finally decides he must leave. Farfrae says sentimentally that now they have something to think about when they are alone. He refers to the incident of the young man and his father. Both of them become slightly uneasy and blush. They both know that something has happened between them. By now Farfrae has completely forgotten the reason that he had come. As he leaves, he promises to come again. Lucetta watches him walk across the market place.

A few minutes later, the maid announces that the Mayor has come. "And he's afraid he hasn't much time to spare, he says," she adds.

"Oh! Then tell him that, as I have a headache, I won't detain him today," Lucetta replies. She hears him leave.

Thinking about Elizabeth-Jane, she suddenly realizes that she can use her as a watchdog to keep her father away since she has no further use for him. When Elizabeth-Jane comes home, Lucetta is again very friendly to her.

Comment

Lucetta, like Henchard and everyone else in Casterbridge, takes an immediate liking to Farfrae. Characteristically, she does something about it. She brazenly plays on Farfrae's sentimentality in a way that Elizabeth-Jane never could because it is essentially dishonest. She flirts with him and actively tries to get him interested. That is not difficult, of course. Here, she is again like Henchard. She, too, is sowing the seeds of her own destruction through her own character. Instead of letting things develop naturally, she insists upon forcing them.

CHAPTER XXIV

For both Lucetta and Elizabeth-Jane, the view out the window on market day was the high point of the week and for the same reason: both hoped to get a glimpse of Donald Farfrae.

One market morning a parcel from London arrives. It contains two dresses one of which Lucetta has to select for her new spring outfit. With Elizabeth-Jane's help, she chooses the cherry-colored one in preference to a pastel. Just after Lucetta puts it on, a new sensation occurs in the marketplace. It is the appearance of a horse-drill; a kind of automatic sower, the first of its type ever seen in Wessex. All the natives gather around it, joking and gawking at the contraption. It is painted bright red, green and yellow and resembles a combination of hornet, grasshopper and shrimp, greatly enlarged.

The two women go out to get a closer look. As they examine it, Henchard appears. He says an embarrassed good morning to Elizabeth-Jane. She, in turn, nervously introduces him to Miss Templeman. They exchange pleasantries. Henchard ridicules the machine briefly and then leaves. As he goes, he mutters a reproach to Lucetta, much to his daughter's astonishment. She decides afterward that she must have imagined it.

Donald Farfrae emerges from the interior of the machine. It was he, they learn, who advised its purchase. He says Henchard is wrong; that this machine will revolutionize sowing. Even though, as Elizabeth-Jane points out, it will destroy the romance of the sower, he defends it in the name of progress. Then he turns to Lucetta. They look at each other ignoring the others. Then the women return inside.

Later, they are talking. Lucetta, who seems to rely on her companion for advice, tells her about her relationship with Henchard and her new attraction to Farfrae. She does not reveal the names, however. She describes it as a problem of a friend. Elizabeth-Jane says it would take a Pope to know what was right. She pities the woman who went through so much suffering. Lucetta also asks how she has been looking. Elizabeth-Jane truthfully answers she looks quite worn. Lucetta bemoans the passing of her good looks. In bed that night, Elizabeth-Jane weeps for Lucetta, knowing that she will not trust her with the real story. She has guessed that Lucetta is the woman in it, but nothing else.

Comment

Elizabeth-Jane has now assumed much the same relationship with Lucetta that Farfrae had with Henchard; she is her adviser and confidante. Just as Farfrae had advised Henchard on business matters, Elizabeth-Jane is asked for advice on matters of dress. Lucetta also feels a compulsion to talk, as Henchard did, and she also unburdens herself to a comparative stranger; and Elizabeth-Jane, like Farfrae, is at a loss to advise about such complicated moral problems. She has never encountered them herself. However, she and Farfrae are not exactly parallel. Elizabeth-Jane is basically imaginative and sensitive whereas Farfrae is at heart a businessman; sentimental, but not very deep in his feelings. This is demonstrated by his defense of mechanical progress against the "romance of the sower."

THE MAYOR OF CASTERBRIDGE

. . . .

CHAPTER XXV

Farfrae comes to call on Lucetta. Both of them, for propriety's sake, pretend that they want Elizabeth-Jane in on the tete-a-tete. They are hardly aware of her existence, however. She quickly contrives to be excused and is not missed. After that, she realizes with heartache that Farfrae is the second man in Lucetta's story.

Henchard comes to call again. He, too, has fallen under Lucetta's spell; even more than before. He feels awkward in her drawing room because Lucetta has become a lady and he isn't sure how to act in such elegant surroundings. He tells her he is ready to do right by her. She replies evasively that there is plenty of time. He says she makes it difficult for him now that she is rich. He reminds her that she can silence her enemies in Jersey by marrying him. She answers only that she will think about it. That instant she glances out the window and sees Farfrae going to market. Fortunately, Henchard does not notice her expression. He leaves saying he cannot understand women. Why did she come to Casterbridge in the first place if not to marry him, he asks himself.

After he is gone, Lucetta comes to a decision. She will break with Henchard and love Farfrae. "I will love him!" she cries.

It is not long before Elizabeth-Jane figures out the true situation. She finds herself back in her former state; ignored by everyone and, rightly, she regretfully decides. For what is she beside Lucetta? She tries to put Farfrae out of her mind and take her misfortunes in stride.

Comment

Henchard is now exactly in the same position that he was when Susan arrived in Casterbridge. A strange woman is in the town, one whom he had a wronged years ago, and to whom he now offers to make amends. But this time there is a difference. Lucetta is not Susan. Her refusal is another sign that Henchard is no longer able to control his destiny.

CHAPTER XXVI

Sometime later, Henchard and Farfrae meet accidentally. Henchard is reading a letter from Lucetta putting off the interview he had asked for. He and Farfrae nod coolly. He asks Farfrae if he remembers the story of the young woman he had wronged. Farfrae replies that he does. Henchard then tells him he has offered to marry her and she has refused. "Well, ye owe her nothing more now," answers Farfrae. Henchard finds, to his anger, that he still wants Lucetta. Finally, he comes to call and she has to see him. He thinks she is after someone else but he cannot discover who it is. As they sit at tea, Farfrae enters. An awkward situation develops. They talk stiffly and nervously ... like children. Elizabeth-Jane, from her objective viewpoint, thinks they are all ridiculous.

Henchard decides he must crush Farfrae in business. To this end, he looks up Joshua Jopp who is still in Casterbridge. He lives in Mixen Lane; in the worst section of town. He readily agrees when Henchard asks him to take over as his manager. He bears a grudge against Farfrae and is eager to help his employer ruin him. Elizabeth-Jane feels so strongly about Jopp that she tells Henchard of her apprehensions; but she is rebuffed.

Henchard and Jopp concoct a scheme to destroy Farfrae. It is based on speculation in wheat prices. They are set up so that if there is a good harvest and wheat is plentiful, prices will be low. If the reverse is true, prices will be extremely high. Since the weather in the spring has been bad, Henchard decides to gamble that it will be bad at harvest time, thus destroying the crop and creating high prices for those who have wheat to sell.

To be sure, however, he goes to a weather prophet in a lonely village in the area. The man claims that he can cure diseases, charm away warts, and perform other magic tricks as well as predict the weather. Henchard gives him money. He predicts that the end of August (harvest time) will be "rain and tempest." Sure now, Henchard buys all the old grain he can get his hands on for the next few weeks. He stores it in his warehouses to sell after the bad harvest.

Almost on signal, the weather changes. It becomes perfect for growing and harvesting. Prices rush downward; a good harvest is almost certain. Henchard sells at once to avoid being ruined altogether. He sells everything for a few shillings on the pound. Even so, he is forced to borrow from the bank and much of his property is rumored to belong to creditors now. Meeting Jopp after he leaves the bank, Henchard savagely blames him for all his misfortunes. Jopp says it was Henchard's idea. After a bit more argument, Henchard fires Jopp. "You shall be sorry for this, sir; sorry as a man can be!" Jopp cries and disappears into the crowd.

CHAPTER XXVII

It is the eve of Harvest. Farfrae, feeling that the other dealers are going overboard on their predictions of a fine harvest, buys up a good deal of old grain at the extremely depressed prices. The harvest starts in perfect weather. Within three days, however, the weather changes again. It begins to rain intermittently and it stays this way. It will not be a disastrous harvest, but, neither will it be a good one. Farfrae makes a large profit even so because he bought the grain at such a low price. As for Henchard, he realizes that, as usual, he acted too soon. Had he waited, at least he would have been able to break even.

One night, a wagon of Henchard's collides with one of Farfrae's near High Place House. The two drivers begin fighting. Henchard's driver was in the wrong but refuses to admit it; especially since he has overturned his wagon. Henchard is called. He accuses the other driver but Lucetta comes out and tells him it was his driver's fault. Henchard decides he must talk to her but she has gone back inside. He asks for her but is refused admittance because she has another appointment. In a fit of jealousy, Henchard waits to see who it is.

The caller is Farfrae. He and Lucetta walk out to the fields where, it being one of the rare good nights, the whole town is working to bring in the crop. Henchard follows them and eavesdrops. His suspicions that Lucetta really loves Farfrae are confirmed by their conversation. He rushes back to wait for her in her house.

She is frightened when she finds him there. Henchard says he has to remind her of a little matter. He wants to know why she has refused to marry him. She pleads to be left alone. She says she doesn't care for him any longer because he wants to marry her out of charity.

He chard demands to know why she came to Casterbridge. After more arguing, Henchard bluntly threatens her that, if she does not promise to marry him, he will tell Farfrae about their affair. He calls in Elizabeth-Jane to be the witness. Lucetta is forced to agree. Elizabeth-Jane, who does not understand why she is agreeing, protests. Henchard asks her what she is complaining about. He says it will now leave Farfrae free for her. Lucetta, miserable, faints and then revives. She refuses, however, to tell Elizabeth-Jane how she came to know Henchard and why he has such power over her.

Comment

One of Henchard's worst failings is his habit of combining business and personal affairs. He is so emotional that a problem in one area always seems to have repercussions in everything else he does. This is just the opposite of Farfrae who keeps his emotional and business lives separate.

Henchard's judgment is always impaired by his violent emotions. He only takes advice that supports what he already believes. He unfairly blames Jopp and the weather-prophet for his misfortunes because, in reality, he had only engaged them to hear his own opinions repeated. Finally, when everything else has failed, Henchard resorts to force. It is the way he knows best. He created a large business because he was more energetic that the others and he feels that this quality is all he needs to get his way in personal matters. It is noteworthy that, in this, he never considers the possibility of being taken in. When he makes Lucetta promise to marry him, the matter is settled ... to his mind. It never occurs to him that she might not carry it out.

CHAPTER XXVIII

The next day, Henchard goes to town hall to preside over the court sessions. Since the current mayor is out of town, Henchard is acting magistrate. There is only one case. A very old, bedraggled woman (recently arrived in the town) has been accused of committing a nuisance in the church. The constable gives evidence; the woman keeps interrupting with fine points of law. She has been in court so many times she knows the procedure better than the Casterbridge officials. Henchard finally tells the constable to stop and asks the old woman if she has anything to say. She begins, "Twenty years ago, I was selling of furmity in a tent at Weydon Fair - A man and a woman with a little child came into my tent...." She goes on to tell the story of the sale. She then says (after the clerks object) "That bears on the case. It proves that he's no better than I, and has no right to sit there in judgment upon me." The clerks do not believe in but Henchard tells them it is true. "'Tis true as the light," he says slowly. "And upon my soul, it does prove that I'm no better than she!" He leaves the court.

The story is a sensation. Soon, word of it comes to Lucetta who is greatly upset over the character of the man she has promised to marry. She decides to go away to the seaside for a few days. Henchard comes to call, a few days later, and is told she has returned but is out for a walk.

Comment

Here is another incident that appears highly coincidental on the surface. Why should the furmity woman come to Casterbridge and why should Henchard happen to be presiding at court the day she is tried? The answer is that her return is symbolic. It is Henchard's guilty past coming back to haunt him again. She is like his conscience; telling him that he is no better than the worst denizen of the slums of Casterbridge. It is Henchard who is being tried in the court of his own conscience. To his credit, he does not attempt to deny his guilt.

CHAPTER XXIX

Lucetta is walking along the road to Port-Bredy; the very place where she has just spent her short vacation. She is obviously looking for someone. Seeing no one ahead, she glances back and spins Elizabeth-Jane walking toward her. She is somewhat annoyed by the intrusion. Before she can say anything, she notices a large and ferocious bull coming up a side path toward them. It appears quite savage. They realize, from the stake dangling behind it, that it has escaped. Becoming frightened, they run into a nearby barn. However, their fright merely encourages the animal and he charges after them. Without realizing what they are doing, they trap themselves inside the barn with the bull. Dashing from side to side, they manage to dodge it. Soon they become tired but, before anything unpleasant happens, a man enters the barn, grabs the stake, wrenches the bull to the ground, and makes him fast. Their rescuer, they now see, is Henchard.

Henchard helps them out of the barn. Since he clearly came after Lucetta and wants to talk to her, Elizabeth-Jane tactfully offers to return to the barn to find Lucetta's muff. At the barn, she finds Farfrae. He has just driven up from the opposite direction. Elizabeth-Jane immediately realizes that he was supposed to meet Lucetta on the road. She informs him of the circumstances of Lucetta's escape from danger. He gives her a ride back but he does not attempt to overtake Lucetta and Henchard. He drops Elizabeth-Jane off and returns home. A number of packed boxes indicate that he is soon moving from his present quarters.

As Henchard and Lucetta return, they discuss their relationship. Henchard tells her that he doesn't want to force her. He is willing to put off the marriage for a year or two ... a kind of indefinite engagement. Lucetta asks if there is anything she can do to thank him for saving her life. Her question comes as a surprise to Henchard. He ponders. Finally, he says that she could come with him to his largest creditor, a man named Grower. Grower knows Lucetta is wealthy and, if they told him that they were getting married in two weeks, Grower would not press for payment of his debts.

Lucetta says she cannot do what Henchard asks. He angrily asks why not. She tells him that she was married to Farfrae in Port-Bredy a few days ago. Grower, by coincidence, was their witness. Henchard is stunned. Lucetta explains tearfully that she is deeply in love with Farfrae. She had heard the story about Henchard selling his wife and thought she could not trust the secret of her past to a man who would do something like that. She felt she had to secure Farfrae or Henchard would ruin her chances.

BRIGHT NOTES STUDY GUIDE

Henchard is very upset. "Then it is his wife's life I have saved this afternoon," he cries. Lucetta offers to help repay his debts but he tells her to go home.

Comment

The fantastic events of this chapter have led many critics to feel that Hardy overdid it a bit. He probably felt that he had to put in a little action for the periodical readers and so invented the wild bull. Even so, it is one of the weakest devices in the novel. It would not have been too difficult to find another way for Henchard to learn of the marriage. We do get a good illustration of Lucetta's character, however, as an indirect consequence of the incident. She, like Henchard, is a schemer and, yet, she is somewhat honest about it. She comes right out and says that the only way she could trap Farfrae was through a secret marriage. She believes that a good end justifies unsavory means.

CHAPTER XXX

Lucetta, by a strenuous effort, gets her emotions under control when Farfrae comes to the house. They discover that neither of them has told Elizabeth-Jane about their marriage. Lucetta says that she should still live with them. Farfrae does not mind but he feels she may not want to.

Lucetta goes upstairs to break the news to her companion. Elizabeth-Jane asks her what is going on in town for she hears wedding bells ringing. Lucetta answers vaguely. She asks Elizabeth-Jane if she remembers the story she told her about her friend and the two men. Elizabeth-Jane replies that she remembers Lucetta had said she was, in honor, bound to marry the first man.

The case is more complicated than that, Lucetta replies. She says that she can no longer trust the first man. She is afraid of him. In that case, Elizabeth-Jane says, she must remain single; Lucetta must marry only Elizabeth-Jane's father (for she has guessed the people involved) or no one.

In saying this, Elizabeth-Jane reveals her almost vicious craving for propriety. Due to the irregularities of her mother's relationship with Newson, she reacts so strongly against moral failings that her standards are fantastically strict. Remembering the bells, she suddenly realizes that Lucetta has gotten married. She instinctively decides, however, that she has done the honorable thing and married Henchard. Lucetta, in great distress, tells her it is someone else. Elizabeth-Jane then realizes she has married Farfrae. Lucetta asks her to remain and live with them. Elizabeth-Jane says she will think about it but, as soon as Lucetta has gone, she prepares to leave. She is unable to approve morally of the marriage; aside from the impossibility of living in the same house as her former lover. She plans to make her way alone; living from the small annuity given her by Henchard and her skill at netting.

Comment

One of the essential conflicts of the book is dramatized in the reaction of Elizabeth-Jane to the news. She represents unbending morality; stiff-necked righteousness that leaves no provision for happiness after a mistake has been made. In this, she is the representative of conventional morality in its strictest form.

We see that, for all her goodness, she has a blind spot too just as does Farfrae, to a greater extent. She, like most fanatics on any subject, is so utterly convinced of her rightness that she makes weaker people doubt their actions. Instead of sympathizing with Lucetta, she accuses her of immorality thus causing her additional anguish. Hardly draws a perfect psychological portrait of Elizabeth-Jane. This is the first time in the novel that she appears so inhumanly proper. Subconsciously, it is not her principles so much as her vanity which has been affronted. If Lucetta had married anyone else by Farfrae, her reaction would undoubtedly have been less severe.

CHAPTER XXXI

In one day, everyone in Casterbridge knows the story of Henchard's past. He soon becomes unwanted socially. At the same time, because of some questionable dealing on the part of one of his men, he loses more money.

In a short time, he is bankrupt. The creditors meet at the bank with Henchard. He empties the money from his pockets and offers them everything he has including his watch. They complement him sympathetically on his honesty.

Elizabeth-Jane goes to look for him but he will see no one. He moves from the big house into Jopp's cottage on the edge of town where Jopp, with great satisfaction, has agreed to take him in. Coming back from a fruitless attempt to see him, Elizabeth-Jane passes his former yards. They have recently been bought by Farfrae. Abel Whittle tells her that, even though Farfrae pays less, it is worth it because he is no longer afraid to come to work.

CHAPTER XXXII

There are two bridges in the lower part of Casterbridge. These bridges usually attract those people who are no longer successful or happy for one reason or another. Henchard often goes to the farther bridge, out of the sight of the town buildings, to meditate on his fate. One day, Jopp passes by there and informs him, spitefully, that Farfrae has purchased his former house and furniture. A few minutes later, Farfrae himself comes by. He asks Henchard if it is true that he is thinking of emigrating. Henchard says yes; both of them appreciate the **irony** of the situation. It is the exact reverse of that of a while ago when Henchard asked Farfrae the same question. Farfrae offers to let him stay in his old house with him and Lucetta. He even offers to return his furniture for nothing. Henchard is touched but he refuses.

Farfrae gets a bad cold and Elizabeth-Jane, hearing about it, insists upon nursing him back to health. In that way, they become friendly again. Henchard finally applies for a job as a hay-trusser at Farfrae's yard. He is taken on. He forgets his jealousy of Farfrae until it is rumored that Farfrae is to become mayor. Then, Henchard undergoes a moral change and, for some mysterious reason, begins counting the days toward something. When he reaches the last day, the mystery is solved with a vengeance. His oath has run out and Henchard begins to drink again.

Comment

Henchard's ruin is now complete. At the same time, Farfrae becomes greater because of it. He seems to be taking over Henchard's very personality. First, he buys his yards; then his house and furniture. He has already taken Henchard's intended wife. It may well be that his dislike of Henchard subconsciously leads him to rub it in this way. There can really be no other explanation for his doing things which could only hurt Henchard deeply. The possibility of Farfrae becoming mayor, and possessing the one mark of distinction that Henchard has had to himself, is part of the process.

CHAPTER XXXIII

It happens to be on a Sunday that Henchard's twenty years are up. He goes to the Three Mariners where it is the custom on Sunday afternoons for the tradesmen of the town to gather for a single half-pint after the weekly church sermon. Henchard is already slightly drunk when the men arrive. He asks them to sing a psalm; insisting upon one which condemns a rich man for his ill gotten wealth and which ends, "And the next age his hated name shall utterly deface."

Farfrae and Lucetta pass by outside. Henchard tells the group that Farfrae is the man about whom they were singing. They tell Henchard he is wrong about him. Henchard says he could crush Farfrae with his bare hands. "And yet I don't" he adds reflectively. Elizabeth-Jane comes to take him home. She becomes alarmed by his half-threats and mutterings about Farfrae but says nothing.

One day, Farfrae brings Lucetta into the yard. Elizabeth-Jane is working there also, Lucetta is surprised to see them. Henchard treats her with sarcastic deference, embarrassing her greatly. Afterward, she sends him a bitter note asking him to leave them alone. After a period of time, Henchard becomes nothing more than another employee to Farfrae. He conceals his bitterness but Elizabeth-Jane knows he feels it more than ever. She decides that she had better warn Farfrae that Henchard may do something rash.

Comment

The fact that Farfrae has accepted Henchard back, under what must be humiliating circumstances, reinforces the opinion that Farfrae is at best unfeeling, or at worst, subconsciously determined to punish Henchard. He should have known better, if he is really a sensitive person; just as Henchard should have known better than to humiliate Abel Whittle.

CHAPTER XXXIV

Elizabeth-Jane meets Farfrae and warns him about Henchard. Farfrae is inclined to take her word lightly. He cannot understand why Henchard would want to do anything to him. He revises his opinion somewhat when others tell him Henchard hates him. He has started a plan to set Henchard up in a small shop with the assistance of other members of the town council but, when they warn him about Henchard, he decides to let it drop. The news comes to Henchard in the form that Farfrae is responsible for his not getting the shop. This adds to his resentment.

At home, Farfrae discusses the matter with Lucetta. He wonders why Henchard should hate him so bitterly. "It's more like an old-fashioned rivalry in love than just a bit of rivalry in trade," he says. Lucetta becomes worried. She wonders whether, perhaps, they could go and live somewhere else. As they are discussing this possibility, one of the town aldermen comes to call.

He tells them that the present mayor has died and that the other aldermen would like to put Farfrae up for the post. Farfrae demurs; saying that he is too young and the others would think he was too pushy. In the end, however, he is convinced to rue. That ends all talk of moving away.

Lucetta seeks out Henchard and asks for the return of her letters. Henchard has forgotten all about them. In fact, he has left them in the safe in his old house. In due time, Farfrae is elected mayor. The next night, Henchard comes to his house to retrieve the letters. He asks Farfrae if he remembers the story. Farfrae does and asks what has happened to the woman. She married well, answers Henchard. He then reads some of the letters to Farfrae who is not really interested but listens politely. They are wildly passionate and loving. Farfrae asks why Henchard didn't marry the woman when Susan died. Learning that she had married another, he says, "The young lady must have had a heart that bore transplanting very readily!"

"She had, she had," answers Henchard. He reads one or two more letters intending to provoke a grand **catastrophe** by revealing Lucetta's name at the conclusion of his reading. When the moment comes, however, he cannot bring himself to do it. He simply cannot be that cruel.

CHAPTER XXXV

Lucetta, hearing someone come in, wonders who it can be at this late hour. From her bedroom, she can make out someone reading something aloud. Curious, she descends the stairs until she can hear more clearly. Suddenly she recognizes Henchard's voice and what he is reading. Paralyzed, she listens for a moment and rushes upstairs sobbing hysterically. Praying that Henchard has not revealed her name, she awaits her husband. When he comes up, she sees that he knows nothing yet. She decides she must fight back and that the best way would be to try to cajole Henchard into returning the letters to her.

She makes an appointment with him for the next night. They are to meet at the Ring; in the very spot where Henchard first met Susan when she came to Casterbridge. Intending to play on his pity and susceptibility to feminine tricks, she dresses plainly and without much makeup.

Henchard is influenced by her disguise. He asks why she looks to worn. She says that he has done it and she asks for the letters. Between the memories the place has for him and the distress Lucetta shows, he is trapped by his own feelings of shame. A man does not persecute weak women. He agrees that he will send the letters the next morning. He adds that, sooner or later, Farfrae will find out about the affair on his own, however. Lucetta replies that by then she hopes to have shown herself a dutiful and loving wife. "I hope so," replies Henchard, dubiously.

Comment

The affair of the letters is another example of Henchard's penchant for grand emotional scenes and his inability to carry them off if they will hurt someone; but, because he is driven to begin such actions, he is powerless to stop them from coming to their conclusions. Lucetta will suffer and die because of his reading the letters despite the fact that he pulled back at the last second. His intentions betray her as much as his actions do. We should also note that it is Farfrae's ambition which triggers Henchard's request for the letters.

CHAPTER XXXVI

Returning home, Lucetta finds Jopp waiting for her outside her door. He asks her to recommend his employment to Farfrae. Lucetta says coldly that she has never seen Jopp before. He informs her that he knows her from Jersey but she still refuses to have anything to do with him. He leaves in anger at his imagined mistreatment.

At his cottage, Henchard asks Jopp to do a favor for him. He gives him the parcel of letters to be delivered to Mrs. Farfrae. After Henchard has retired, Jopp opens the package and finds the letters. He does not read them, however, but puts them under his arm and then sets off to do as Henchard has asked.

On the way, he meets Mrs. Cuxsom and Nance Mockridge. They invite him to come to Peter's Finger, an inn in Mixen Lane; the vice row of Casterbridge. He accepts. At the inn, all the various thieves, prostitutes, poachers and swindlers of the area are gathered. They talk and drink. One of the loudest is the furmity-woman who has settled in Mixen Lane for the time being. She asks Jopp what he is carrying. He tells them. For a joke, they open the package and read the letters. They decide that the affair would be a fine foundation for a skimmity-ride.

Just then, someone else arrives followed by a stranger. The second man is new to Casterbridge and, when he comes into the inn, he is taken aback at the kind of people he finds there. Since he is rather richly dressed himself, it is obvious that he has stumbled into the wrong place. However, he good-naturedly buys a drink before he leaves. As he is going, he asks what a skimmity-ride is as he hears them using the term. The landlady replies, "'Tis a foolish thing they do in these parts when a man's wife is - well, not too particularly his own."

The stranger laughs and says he would like to see something like that. It costs money to do, they tell him. He gives them a gold piece to help; then, he departs. Soon afterward, Jopp gathers up the letters and leaves also. The next morning, he delivers them to Lucetta. She promptly and thankfully burns them.

Comment

As in Henchard's case, the lowest class of people brings about the downfall of Lucetta. They make the point that she too is no better than they are. Also, like the furmity woman in Henchard's case, it is someone out of Lucetta's guilty past who is responsible for destroying her. And, by a further curious **irony**, Jopp and Farfrae are both present in Casterbridge for the same reason.

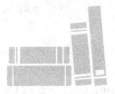

THE MAYOR OF CASTERBRIDGE

....

CHAPTER XXXVII

About this time, a great event in the history of Casterbridge is about to take place. A royal personage is scheduled to pass through the town on his way to the West for the inauguration of a great engineering project. He has consented to stop briefly in Casterbridge. The town excitedly makes preparations.

Henchard determines that he shall take part in the official welcome. He goes to the council and asks if he can do so. Farfrae, as mayor, tells him he is just another journeyman laborer and that he must watch from the side like the rest. Henchard stalks out; muttering that he will welcome the royal visitor despite them.

On the great day, the town worthies, with Farfrae and Lucetta at their head, wait the royal cortege from a stand. Henchard stands below them looking at Lucetta. She is dressed in her best outfit, bursting with snobbery and pride. She gazes over the crowd but shows no sign of knowing Henchard.

The cortege arrives. Suddenly, before anyone can stop him, Henchard steps before the royal carriage and unrolls a home-made flag with his left hand. He offers his right to the royal personage. Everyone is embarrassed. Farfrae rises to the occasion. He seizes Henchard and drags him back into the crowd and tells him to be off. They confront each other briefly but Henchard gives in and leaves.

The ladies with Lucetta remark that the man was Farfrae's old patron. Lucetta snobbishly denies that Henchard ever helped her husband. She meets the royal visitor. Soon, he is gone and Casterbridge can return to normal.

The town idlers stay and talk about the day's events. They also discuss the mayor and his wife. They do not have as much affection for him, now that he has risen in the world, as they did before. Finally, the conversation turns to the proposed skimmity-ride. Christopher Coney and Solomon Longways decide to find out if it will really take place. If it will, they feel they should warn those concerned to keep out of the way, for such things can be quite rough, and Lucetta has done nothing wrong since she came to Casterbridge ... no matter what she did before.

CHAPTER XXXVIII

Henchard, after his removal by Farfrae, has remained at the ceremonies briefly. He has stayed long enough to hear Lucetta deny that he has ever done anything for her husband. This, he feels to be the ultimate insult.

BRIGHT NOTES STUDY GUIDE

Later that day, he is still in a daze over the events. He fingers his coat where Farfrae had seized him as if he cannot yet believe he has been handled by the mayor. Finally, in a fury, he goes to find Farfrae and challenge him to a fight. At Farfrae's house, he leaves a message asking Farfrae to meet him at one of the sheds. He goes there and climbs up to the open third level where he plans to fight to the finish with Farfrae; whichever man can throw the other off will be the victor. Farfrae arrives. He asks, with annoyance, that Henchard is doing. Why hasn't he taken his holiday like the rest of the men? Henchard tells him that now they will finish the wrestling match which Farfrae started in the square that morning. To make it fair, he has tied one hand behind his back. Then, he lunges at Farfrae forcing him to fight for his life.

After a titanic struggle, Henchard succeeds in overpowering Farfrae. He holds him over the ledge, saying, "... This is the end of what you began this morning. Your life is in my hands." "Then take it, take it!" Farfrae replies. "Ye've wished to long enough."

Henchard looks at him. "O Farfrae! - that's not true." he says bitterly. "God is my witness that no man ever loved another as I did thee at one time ... and now ... I cannot hurt thee!" He lets him go. Extremely ashamed, he remains up in the loft in a kind of stupor at how low he has sunk.

Finally, he leaves. He has a great desire to see Farfrae again; to try to explain to him why he acted so crazily but he remembers that, as Farfrae left, Abel Whittle had come and given him a letter. Henchard had heard Farfrae say that he would have to go to Weatherbury and so would be late in getting home. Henchard goes to the bridge instead. While he stands there miserably, he hears a noise from another part of the town. He is so wrapped up in his own thoughts that he ignores it.

Comment

Farfrae has now humiliated Henchard in every way possible. In this final crazy interruption of the ceremony, Henchard forces his rival to lay hands on him. Farfrae has no choice but that does not occur to Henchard. He only knows that he has been physically pushed around by Farfrae. In the one area in which he is demonstrably better than the Scot ... pure brute strength ... he has been bested. To save some small portion of his pride, he makes Farfrae fight him but, when he wins the fight, he realizes that he has not really won since, in doing so, he has lost his last bit of manhood. All he had left was the knowledge that he could beat Farfrae but had chosen not to; now, he hasn't even that.

CHAPTER XXXIX

The letter which Farfrae has received after his battle with Henchard is anonymous. It has been sent by Longways and Coney who have discovered that, indeed, there is to be a skimmity-ride. By sending him to Weatherbury, they hope to get him out of the way so that he will not have to witness it. They have not warned Lucetta since they feel that there was probably some truth to the scandal and that she will have to bear it as best she can.

That night, Lucetta is still glowing in the aftermath of the day's happenings. She notices the same disturbance that Henchard has heard in the previous chapter. It grows louder. Then, she hears two maids talking across the street. One asks the other what is going on. The second replies that it seems to be a skimmity-ride coming up the street. There are two effigies on a donkey, one of a woman facing the front and one of a man facing the rear. Who are they? asks the first, eagerly. The other looks and declares spitefully that the woman is Mrs. Farfrae.

Just then, Elizabeth-Jane rushes in. She goes to close the shutters but it is too late. Lucetta holds her back. She becomes unnerved, shrieking, "Donald will see it….It will break his heart - he will never love me anymore - and oh, it will kill me - kill me." She goes to the window and looks out at the parade. "She's me - she's me - even to the parasol - my green parasol!" she cries wildly. She pauses, motionless for a moment, then crashes unconscious to the floor.

Elizabeth-Jane sends for a doctor, who comes at once; fortunately, he had gone out to see what all the commotion was about. He examines Lucetta. It is a serious fit, he says, because Lucetta's health is not good. He sends for Farfrae.

Meanwhile, Mr. Grower has roused the town constables who have been hiding in fear and comes into the street to find the culprits. They are nowhere to be seen, however. Getting reinforcements, they go to Peter's Finger but everyone there denies hearing a thing. They find a noisemaker but, even though they are sure who is involved, they have no proof.

CHAPTER XL

Henchard has wearied of the bridge and walks into town. On his way, he encounters the skimmity-ride returning. He immediately knows what it is and goes to Farfrae's house. They tell him what has happened. He says that Farfrae has gone to Weatherbury instead of following his original plans to go to Budmouth. They do not believe him. Knowing that Lucetta's life depends upon Farfrae returning, Henchard sets out to find him himself. Running madly, he goes several miles before he sees him. He stops Farfrae's gig and tells him what has happened. Farfrae does not believe him either. He thinks it is a trick designed to give Henchard another chance to make an attempt on his life. Henchard pleads with him. He does not listen and continues on to make a call in a nearby town.

Henchard returns to Casterbridge. Very depressed, he goes back to Jopp's cottage. When he gets there, Jopp tells him that someone was here to see him; a sea-captain of some sort. He has not left a message nor his name. Henchard says, in that case, he will pay it no mind. Later, unable to sleep, he goes out again. He comes to Farfrae's house. By this time, the Scot has returned and has been up with Lucetta all night. Every hour or so, Henchard returns to the house to make inquiries about the patient. On his last call, he sees a servant removing the cloth which has been used to muffle the knocker. He asks why. The reply is, "Because they may knock as loud as they will; she will never hear it anymore."

Comment

Lucetta's past returns to kill her in the form of a symbolic effigy. She recognizes, at the end, that it has been her foolish vanity and pride in her new position which has brought in upon her.

Her death is the conclusion to the second part of the novel. The two guilty characters, Henchard and Lucetta, have been brought low. For both of them, it is the same facets of their characters (which led them to commit their past mistakes) that cause the new catastrophes.

Farfrae, too, has suffered a loss; in his case, the first since he has come to Casterbridge. It is his lack of understanding of Henchard's character as much as the skimmity-ride which accounts for Lucetta's death. He could not know whether Henchard was telling the truth but he should have returned.

CHAPTER XLI

It is now early morning. Henchard goes home. Elizabeth-Jane comes to tell him the news. He asks her to stay and rest. She does so; feeling closer to him than she has in a long time.

While she is sleeping, the stranger, who has sought Henchard the previous night, arrives. He asks if Henchard remembers him. Henchard says no. "Well," the man answers, "Perhaps you may not. My name is Newson." "I know the name well," Henchard answers, slowly.

They discuss Susan. Newson tells him substantially the same story that Susan told concerning their relationship. He adds that, soon after they returned from America and Susan began having qualms about their relationship, he went on a voyage which was wrecked off Newfoundland. He decided to stay there a while so that Susan would think him dead and would try to find Henchard. He stayed in Canada until just a month ago. In Falmouth, they told him Susan is dead; now, he is looking for his daughter.

Henchard impulsively says that she is dead, too. Newson accepts his word and leaves in great sorrow. When he has gone, Henchard realizes that he cannot let matters rest like that. He goes after Newson. Just as he is about to catch up with him, Newson gets into the coach and is gone.

Henchard returns, half expecting that Elizabeth-Jane will have vanished. She is still there; just waking. He tenderly makes breakfast for her. He tells her he is very lonely and she says she will come often. Then, Henchard leaves for work.

All day he is disturbed by the thought that Newson will come back and he will lose Elizabeth-Jane too; just as he has lost Susan, Farfrae, and Lucetta. He feels he has nothing ahead of him but years of loneliness. The thought of such a life becomes unendurable. At the end of the day, he crosses over the bridge and walks to Ten Hatches; a dark, dreary spot along the river. The water there runs deep and swift and, there, he intends to end his life. As he stands looking into the black water, he notices something. To his horror, it is a dead body; dressed in his clothes, resembling him exactly. He returns home under great strain.

At home, he finds Elizabeth-Jane. He takes her to the river and asks her what she sees. Looking hard, she too discerns the effigy. They must have hidden it here after the skimmity-ride, she says. From Henchard's reaction, she guesses his suicidal intentions. She asks him if she can come and live with him again. He assents gratefully; beginning to feel that perhaps he too can be happy.

Comment

With Newson's departure, there is no one left who can cause Henchard any trouble. Despite his fears, there is no reason why Newson should return.

The **episode** at Ten Hatches puts the final seal on the second section of the book. It is a symbol both of Henchard's death and of his life. He has symbolically suffered and died for his crimes and the atonement can end. This is made clearer by Elizabeth-Jane's request to live with him. There is no reason now that he cannot begin life again and be relatively happy for the rest of his days.

CHAPTER XLII

The members of the town council, led by Farfrae, finally purchase a small seed shop for Henchard and his daughter. For the remainder of the year, they run the shop and live above it. Occasionally, Henchard still has fears that Newson will return but nothing much happens to upset the relative tranquility he has found. Farfrae, too, after a period of mourning, begins to resume his former life. He realizes that his life with Lucetta was doomed to have great disappointments in it, had she lived, and he makes the best of what has happened.

Henchard continually cautions himself against being unkind to Elizabeth-Jane for fear that she will leave him again. He notices that she seems to be taking a good many long walks but his fear of offending her keeps him from asking questions. As Spring comes, he becomes suspicious that she is doing something that he does not know about. One day, she comes home with a new muff which he remarks is very expensive. She also seems to be buying a great number of books; more than she can really afford.

One day, he realizes that she always seems to go past Farfrae's position at the exchange on her walks. He immediately suspects that she is involved with the Scot. Any other man he could stand but that perverse instinct which has betrayed Henchard so many times does so again. The idea of Farfrae taking Elizabeth-Jane away from him becomes almost more than he can bear.

He spies on them and his suspicions are confirmed. He sees Farfrae and Elizabeth-Jane kiss and hears him address her as "Dearest Elizabeth-Jane." A violent conflict takes place inside him. On one hand, he thinks that, if he were to tell Farfrae that Elizabeth-Jane was legally no one's child (that she was really illegitimate) the perfectly proper leading citizen would think twice before carrying on with her. On the other hand, he knows it is not right for him to try to interfere with anyone's life. He has caused enough trouble that way already.

CHAPTER XLIII

In a short time, other people in the town notice the courtship of Elizabeth-Jane and talk about it. Some feel that he is lowering himself. The idlers at the Three Mariners feel just the opposite: that he is lucky to get a girl like Elizabeth-Jane.

Nothing is said to Henchard, and he becomes very depressed by the impending nuptials; even his health suffers. He thinks about his alternatives: living as an unwanted guest in Farfrae's house, to be patronized by him and Elizabeth-Jane, or to live in loneliness without her. Both answers are abhorrent to him.

The problem is solved, in the worst possible way, by Newson's return. Henchard's worst fears have now come true. He sees Newson on the road and knows everything is over for him. When he returns home, he prepares to leave Casterbridge forever. He informs Elizabeth-Jane of his decision. She weeps, entreating him to stay, but he will not. He knows that, as soon as she meets Newson, she will despise him. Elizabeth-Jane thinks he is leaving because she is marrying Farfrae. Henchard says she will soon enough know why he is leaving. He asks her to promise that she will not forget him entirely.

That day, Henchard buys some new hay-trussing equipment. He leaves Casterbridge in the evening; striding from the town on the same road on which he had entered it almost a quarter century before.

At the top of the hill, overlooking Casterbridge, he turns and pauses. "If I had only got her with me - if I only had!" he says. "Hard work would be nothing to me then. But that was not to be. I - Cain - go alone as I deserve - an outcast and a vagabond. But may punishment is not greater than I can bear." He turns and trudges on.

Farfrae comes and takes Elizabeth-Jane to his house. Newson is there to greet her. After a tearful reunion, he tells her the true facts of her parentage and Henchard's actions. Farfrae, quite cheerful, insists that Newson live with them after the marriage. Newson agrees. They all decide to put Henchard out of their minds. What's over is over, they say; they have done with him.

Comment

Most critics feel that the final four chapters are the weakest in the novel. Hardy, at this point, seems to have lost interest in his characters. At any rate, the motivations and incidents of these chapters are far less convincing than is true of the earlier sections.

There is really no reason for Henchard to become so upset all over again over Farfrae. The problem of living in his house is somewhat gratuitous since Henchard already has a place to live. Above all, there is no convincing reason for Newson to return. Once he does, it is certainly true that Henchard has no other alternative than to leave. We can also expect Farfrae not to be concerned in such circumstances. However, the lack of sympathy and understanding on the part of Elizabeth-Jane seems somewhat out of character.

CHAPTER XLIV

Henchard walks eastward until he is too weary to go on. He continues walking in this direction for six days; until he comes to Weydon-Priors. He intends to visit the scene of his crime, as a kind of penance, before he searches for work. Standing on the hill in the exact spot where the furmity tent had been, he recalls the parting words of his wife. He experiences not only the bitterness of a man who has learned that ambition has not been worth the price but, also, of a man who has learned to love and repent only to be rejected again.

Although he intends to go on into another part of the country, he cannot bear to be so far from Elizabeth-Jane. Consequently, he turns right and wanders in a wide circle through the countryside with Casterbridge as the center. He thinks of her all the time. Finally, he gets a job hay-trussing some fifty miles from Casterbridge, along the main Western road. He asks travelers from the West if they know anything of the impending wedding. One of them tells him that it is to be very soon.

After much thought, he resolves to attend. He will try once more to make Elizabeth-Jane understand. He spends what little money he has to purchase some better clothes and sets out. On the way, he looks for a suitable present that he can afford. He buys a goldfinch in a plain cage. He arrives in Casterbridge on the wedding day. The marriage has already taken place and now the couple is giving a reception at their home. Henchard does not have the courage to enter through the front door. He goes to the kitchen where he asks the housekeeper to tell Elizabeth-Jane that, "A humble old friend has come." Waiting for her, Henchard looks into the front room where there is dancing. He sees Farfrae dancing and disapproves slightly of all the gaiety. He notices someone else dancing even more vigorously than Farfrae. When the dancer turns to give a full view, he recognizes the man as Newson. He realizes that Newson has completely supplanted him and he turns to go.

Elizabeth-Jane enters the room. He pleads with her almost incoherently. She takes her hand away accusing Henchard of treating her cruelly. She says she cannot love anyone like him. Henchard at once ceases to ask for forgiveness. "Don't ye distress yourself on my account," he says proudly. "I'll never trouble 'ee again, Elizabeth-Jane." He leaves.

Comment

Given the circumstances which now exist, it is reasonable for Henchard to act as he does. The callousness of the others in dropping him so completely is well emphasized by the dancing and festivities at the wedding. It demonstrates the coldness of Farfrae's character. A second marriage, coming not long after the tragic death of his first wife, would not seem quite the time for such joyous celebration. We can believe, however, that Farfrae is capable of such action. What is hard to accept is the indifference of Elizabeth-Jane to both the memory of Lucetta and to Henchard. Her character seems to have undergone a drastic change since Henchard left Casterbridge.

CHAPTER XLV

It is about a month after the wedding. The housekeeper tells Elizabeth-Jane that they have discovered who left that birdcage; the one that had been found in a corner with a starved dead goldfinch in it a few days after the wedding. It was the poor farmer, says the housekeeper.

Elizabeth-Jane begins to think about Henchard. She realizes the birdcage was a wedding gift and feels sorry for the way she treated him. She convinces Farfrae, who doesn't care one way or another, that they must find Henchard and try to help him. They try to trace his path. Following it to Egdon Heath, they come to a series of crossroads. Farfrae says, if they go on, it will cost too much so they must turn back and try again some other time.

Just then, they see Abel Whittle. Amazed that he should be so far from Casterbridge, they alight and follow him. He goes to an old, crumbling cabin. He tells them that he has been minding Henchard who has died a half hour before. He says Henchard was kind to his mother when she was in need and he owed it to him to try to help him when Henchard had no one. He gives them Henchard's will which he cannot read.

The will asks that no one remember or bother about him; even in death. They follow his instructions; sorrowfully on Elizabeth-Jane's part, without emotion on Farfrae's part. From that time on, Elizabeth-Jane's life is the reverse of her earlier days. She is happy in a way that she has never dreamed was possible.

Comment

The starved bird obviously symbolizes Henchard. He, too, has been starved of love and dies. It is significant that, at his death, it is Abel Whittle who ministers to him. Whittle has as much reason as anyone to dislike Henchard. He helps him at the end, however, because Henchard was once kind to Whittle's mother. Henchard was also kind to Farfrae and Elizabeth-Jane at important times in their lives, yet they do not assist him when he needs it most. Both of them are shown to have little human sympathy at the end.

THE MAYOR OF CASTERBRIDGE

Tragic hero ⌐ and worse than greater ordinary people.

MICHAEL HENCHARD

As the title character, Henchard is, by far, the most commanding figure in the novel. He is a tragic hero in the sense that the term is applied to Othello or Oedipus. He is a man larger than life; greater and worse than ordinary people. This is the foundation stone of Henchard's character. His actions and motives are always excessive whether he is engaged in doing good as he often is, or, in being cruel.

He makes faults of things that would ordinarily be virtues because of his tendency to carry them to extremes. Qualities such as honesty, fairness, and courage are so important to him that they sometimes make him too rigid and intolerant. Because he is completely honest, for example, he often offends people by telling them exactly what he thinks. He is unable to understand or conform to common politeness, as he tells Lucetta. He is a plain-spoken and direct man who says what he has to say and no more. In this way, he is quite simple and unsophisticated. Having once decided on a course of action, he immediately proceeds with great energy and ignores the consequences.

He feels emotions more intensely than those of the other characters. This is partly because his ideas and judgments are more perceptive than is normal; but, also, because they are relatively simple and clear-cut. He is always positive that he knows right from wrong, in business or in personal relationships and he always sticks to his judgments. One of his finest qualities is his refusal to forget or talk himself out of what he knows to be true. A lesser man would have discreetly forgotten about Susan after a few years and denied, when the question arose, that he ever knew her before. Henchard cannot.

On the other hand, this elemental simplicity is not always a virtue. Knowing you are always right often leads to rash action which is later regretted. It causes Henchard to be unable to see someone else's side of the picture. It leads him to violent anger and abruptness in cases that are only worsened by such action. Above all, it makes him ill-suited for dealing with people who cannot or will not meet his exacting standards. This, in turn, creates unnecessary difficulties with almost everyone else in his life.

These character faults would not be of crucial importance if they were not combined with another and greater fault: that of excessive pride. Like Othello or Oedipus, he feels intuitively that he is worthier than other people. This feeling is responsible for his dynamic rise in the world, but also for his fall. Because he is a larger person than the others around him, his pride will not let him react like an ordinary human. A minor joke, at his expense, becomes a major insult. When he is depressed, he is almost paralyzed by the intensity of his feelings. He thinks that no one can be neutral where he is concerned. If they do not reciprocate his friendship in the passionate manner in which he usually offers it, they are his enemies; there is no in-between.

It is his pride which finally destroys him. He cannot admit that he has made a mistake until it is too late. He cannot admit that another person, indeed every other person, deserves the same consideration that he demands for himself.

And yet, paradoxically, it is his pride that makes him great and sympathetic to us. He prides himself most on being a man; and he remains true to that ideal. He will not beg to be forgiven when he finally does understand his errors. Although it makes him miserable, he is not afraid to leave Casterbridge and return to a life of menial labor. Above all, he is never afraid to accept the consequences of his mistakes. At the conclusion, he goes away to die alone; without appealing for mercy or assistance from anyone, without crying that he has been misunderstood. In this way, he finally establishes his moral superiority over those who have rejected him.

ELIZABETH-JANE

Henchard's supposed daughter is a good example of how contemporary readers look at a character intended to reflect an ideal of behavior that was current a hundred years ago. To our eyes, along with her many good qualities, she is an extremely repressed, prudish and sometimes difficult young lady. To Victorian eyes, she was a model of decorum, exactly what a young girl was expected to be. There are indications that Hardy, perhaps subconsciously, intended both aspects to be present in her character. He tells us specifically, at one point in chapter 30 and, indirectly, at many others, that her concern for propriety borders on the fanatic. She is so strait-laced, even compared to her contemporaries, that she instinctively condemns anyone who cannot meet her rigid ideas of moral conduct. Usually, she repents her criticism but, by then, the damage has been done.

This blind spot aside, she has many excellent qualities. In most ways, she does deserve Hardy's description of her as a "flower of nature." She is the only truly kind person in the book. She is the only one who goes out of her way to help others consistently. She is genuinely sensitive as well. Excluding Henchard, her emotions are deeper and more heartfelt than anyone else's. She is quite intelligent and observant, in an objective way that is unique. Of all the characters, she is the one with the most sensible, balanced viewpoint on most questions.

All of these characteristics are subservient to another, however. Elizabeth-Jane is, first and foremost, a serious, introspective person. This is what the others notice about her before anything else and what remains her outstanding feature. She is always grave and withdrawn; partly from shyness, partly from a sense of inferiority, partly because it is her natural manner. Along with this, she has a great capacity to suffer; to sacrifice herself. She is entirely without pride or expectations of happiness. She does not fight back but meekly accepts her fate, whatever it may be. Because she is accustomed to waiting, everything comes to her in the end. Her triumph illustrates one of the philosophic statements of the novel.

DONALD FARFRAE

The Scot is another character about whom we feel conflicting sentiments. As with Elizabeth-Jane, Hardy himself seems not to believe completely all the wonderful things he has written about him. When we first see Farfrae, he is presented as a charming, romantic stranger. He is shown to be generous, attractive, soft-spoken, patriotic, and a fine ballad singer. He is also ambitious, clever, a whiz at mechanical inventions and, as we soon learn, a superb businessman. However, something is wrong with this picture. He is, we soon realize, too good to be true.

Hardy makes some of his reservations explicit. The **episode** with the new mechanical sower shows that Farfrae is much more the businessman than the romantic. When he takes over Henchard's grain yards, he immediately lowers the salaries of the employees, which is not the act of a generous man. He is also quite humorless and finds it hard to appreciate harmless joking.

For the most part, however, he has the good qualities which everyone claims for him. Despite this, he lacks the one quality that Henchard has in greatest measure: depth and intensity of feeling. Farfrae is shallow. His good manners, his patriotism, his ambition are of the most conventional, sentimental kind) He is sincere and well-meaning but he does not understand anyone whose character is different from his. He does not realize how much he has hurt Elizabeth-Jane by dropping her so suddenly for Lucetta. Even his love for Lucetta is shown to be shallow by the ease with which he gets over her death.

Above all, he cannot understand Henchard. Although everything that Farfrae does is perfectly reasonable, he is often unintentionally cruel. He does not realize that Henchard will be insulted by his giving an entertainment on the holiday. He does not understand that the most degrading thing he can do the Henchard is to buy his house and furniture. Finally, he does not believe Henchard is sincere on the road to Weatherbury and so insures Lucetta's death.

Farfrae triumphs over Henchard not because he is a better person but because his qualities are perfectly suited for success in the world of Casterbridge and Henchard's are not. Farfrae is a perfect product of a society in which superficial values are the standard. We would not consider him to be so perfect today. Hardy, at least subconsciously, may well have felt the same way when he was creating him.

LUCETTA

Of all the characters in the novel, Lucetta is the least English. She is dark and sensual in appearance, like Henchard, whereas all the others are fair and proper. As we know from her name, she is not even English by birth or descent. Her character is almost a stereotype of the Englishman's opinion of continental Europeans, particularly Latins. She is emotional and impulsive, given to quick decisions and reversals. Along with that, she is earthy and sexually exciting; something no proper English- woman was allowed to be at the time. She gives in to her emotions when an Englishwoman would control herself. She is weak and flighty and devotes a great deal of time to making herself attractive to men. In short, she is completely feminine and pays no attention to such notions as improving her mind or being dignified. Although she tries to make herself English, she cannot. In the end, her passionate nature betrays her. Within these limitations, however, she is a decent person. As far as she is capable, she has sympathy for others and tries to assist them if he can. Her good intentions are always thwarted by her own character, however; first, by her lack of perception and, finally, by her basic lack of concern for others.

SUSAN HENCHARD

Susan's character is virtually one-dimensional. She is passive, weak, and long-suffering; a kind of sounding board against which Henchard can be judged. Only rarely does she show signs of anything but meek acceptance of her lot. Her only other important characteristic, besides a tired bitterness toward the world, is her fervent love for her daughters. She acquiesces in the sale mainly for the original Elizabeth-Jane's sake, and she dares to lie to Henchard about the second for love of her. This is almost the only act in her life which shows a spirit of independence. In everything else she is afraid. She is completely ordinary in every way. Moral problems confuse her; life in general confuses her. She cannot cope with it and looks forward to her death. The next world cannot treat her worse than this one.

NEWSON

The sailor is another more or less stock character. He is kindly, jolly, and sympathetic. He is also quite simple and trusting which is shown by his immediate acceptance of Henchard's lie. Most of all, he is easy-going. He takes life as it happens without worrying too much about it. Hardy uses him mainly to help the plot along and as a comparison to Henchard.

JOSHUA JOPP

Jopp is the time-tested villain. His character is little more than a mean and nasty outlook on life. When he is slighted, he wants revenge but hasn't the strength of character to do anything but curse and gossip. He tries to blackmail Lucetta and is brushed off as insignificant. This is a true estimate of his character, a nasty, stupid, incompetent bother. He does strongly influence the plot, of course, but even the skimmity-ride is not originally his idea. He causes it only by accident; although he enthusiastically supports the suggestion as a way of getting even.

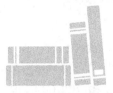

THE MAYOR OF CASTERBRIDGE

CRITICAL COMMENTARY

The Mayor of Casterbridge is one of the most difficult of Hardy's novels. It has been highly praised, and just as loudly condemned, by critics. While there is general agreement on the value of, for example, *The Return of the Native*, or *Tess of the D'Urbervilles*, this has not been the case with *The Mayor of Casterbridge*. What is more, some critics who have liked the novel have done so for the very reasons that others have disliked it; and, vice versa.

In general, Hardy criticism can be divided into two periods; each period has a very different point of view. The first we can call Victorian and post-Victorian, meaning critics who, for the most part, were younger contemporaries of Hardy. The second we can call modern, meaning critics who are for the most part writing today. There are, of course, a good many years separating the two groups. Even more important than time, however, are their quite opposite attitudes toward literature. Both groups do agree that Hardy is a great writer but that is all that they agree upon.

EARLIER CRITICISM

Turn of the century critics like Lionel Johnson, Samuel Chew, and Lascelles Abercrombie praised Hardy for his **realism**. Thus, when they talked about *The Mayor of Casterbridge*, they pointed out, as its strongest points, the perfect descriptions of the Wessex countryside, the detailed accounts of the daily goings-on in Casterbridge, the exactly reproduced dialects of the natives, and so on. These critics felt that the proper artistic method for a novelist was to try to reproduce life exactly as it would be seen in a photograph. If there were a table in a room, for example, they wanted to know its size in inches and feet, what was on it, how old it was, how many scratches it had, and so on. When they criticized him, it was for creating incidents too far-fetched to be quite believable. They also admonished him for being pessimistic which they considered a false, unjustified outlook on life.

Another point they praised was Hardy's philosophizing. They automatically assumed that the point of his novels was to deliver a moral message. Although Hardy often said that he was not trying to present a definite statement about life, his early critics felt that every novelist had to do this. After all, they felt, what was the good of literature if it did not teach the reader something? Hardy believed this also, to some extent, although not nearly as much as did his critics.

These first critics also considered Hardy a great "writer," in the technical sense. Johnson called him a "master craftsman," meaning that his choice of words, construction of sentences and, indeed, whole books was of the highest order.

MODERN CRITICISM

The moderns, the most important of whom is Albert J. Guerard of Harvard, tell a different story. They say that the qualities praised by Johnson and the others are the worst, not the best, qualities in Hardy's work. To judge *The Mayor of Casterbridge* in realistic terms is foolish, they claim. How could a story as full of fantastic coincidences as *The Mayor of Casterbridge* be considered a realistic portrayal of life in rural England in the 1840s? In real life anywhere conversations are not invariably overheard, kind sailors do not appear at the right moment and buy wives, the weather does not always change just at the proper moment, bulls do not escape and chase young ladies, and so on. Hardy may be realistic in the smaller things but certainly not in the more important.

They go on to say that Hardy was not much of a philosopher either. Guerard calls his ideas "often commonplace" and points out that there was nothing at all original in them. He goes on to say that Hardy's "messages" are not very profound; moreover, very often he wasn't really concerned with making a philosophical point. He was a poet and storyteller first, a thinker second.

Finally, modern critics feel that often Hardy was a very bad "writer." His descriptive passages are sometimes very clumsy. There are sections in all his novels which are extremely dull and tedious to read. Sometimes, as in the last four chapters of *The Mayor of Casterbridge*, he seems to lose interest. Many of his works are extremely uneven. Novels which begin wonderfully, like *A Laodicean* or *Two on a Tower*, fall apart after a few chapters. Much of this can be ascribed to the fact that his novels were usually serialized in magazines and, so, written in sections. Even so, it seems that Hardy, more than most important writers, had his ups and downs in inspiration.

Why, then, do modern critics consider Hardy a great writer? Why, in particular, do they consider *The Mayor of Casterbridge* one of Hardy's two great novels? (The other is *Jude the Obscure*.)

PSYCHOLOGICAL ASPECTS

The first answer to that question can be hinted at by asking ourselves what kind of book *The Mayor of Casterbridge* really is. If it is not primarily a realistic story of mid-19th century country life in West England, what is it? Our first answer is that it is primarily a novel about a single person, Michael Henchard. Furthermore, it is a novel about the psychology of Michael Henchard. Instead of looking at his life from the outside, like a photograph, Hardy is concerned with the mind of his major character.

Hardy said, in the novel, that "character is fate." Modern critics, with a knowledge of psychology, point out that character is not consistent or logical. There is no guarantee that people will act logically or do what they know to be sensible. They are often foolish and irrational despite themselves. A person like Michael Henchard is especially inconsistent. If we realize this, many of the apparent awkward coincidences and illogicalities of behavior become acceptable. We see that, often, these coincidences are actually caused by Henchard and are just the kind of thing we would except of a person with his psychological makeup. He "accidentally" meets Farfrae on the morning the Scot is to leave for Bristol; he "coincidentally" gives Jopp the letters to take to Lucetta instead of delivering them himself; he just "happens" to be nearby when the wagons crash and so meets Lucetta; etc., etc.

Many of the odd things that Henchard does, and which later have a crucial effect on the story, can be seen as perfectly consistent from the psychological point of view. Why does Henchard give the letters to Jopp, for example? If it is only because Hardy needs it to help along the plot, it is not very convincing but, it we consider that Henchard unconsciously probably still bears a grudge against Lucetta, it is not unreasonable that he would give Jopp the letters. Jopp has reason to dislike both Henchard and Lucetta. Henchard may well be unconsciously hoping that Jopp will revenge himself by not following Henchard's instructions; thereby hurting Lucetta.

The idea that Henchard's unconscious drives him to certain actions, and to make certain decisions against his better judgment, is the greatest departure modern critics make from the post-Victorian viewpoint. They call *The Mayor of Casterbridge* a "Freudian" novel in the sense that it is about the psychology, both conscious and unconscious, of its characters. To reply that the book was written years before anyone heard of Freud, does not change their opinion. It shows that Hardy, like Dostoevsky and Flaubert, was an acute enough student of human nature to have anticipated Freud's discoveries.

Henchard's unconscious guilt feelings over the sale of his wife are central to the novel. If we assume that he tries unconsciously to punish himself for his misdeed, it helps account for many more of his irrational decisions and desires. His foolish business risks, or indeed his fanatic drive to destroy Farfrae in general, are best understood if considered from this angle. We know, from the beginning of the novel, that he will not be able to overcome Farfrae; rather, that the opposite is inevitable and he will be destroyed by the Scot. Perhaps unconsciously, Henchard knows this too. In forcing Farfrae to fight him he is unconsciously insuring his own humiliation and punishment.

This is not unusual, according to modern psychology. A person with deeply suppressed guilt feelings is often driven to seek punishment for his guilt. Henchard, to modern critics, is an excellent example of such a case.

Although Henchard is the major figure, it is also possible to explain the single most inconsistent action of Elizabeth-Jane by referring to her unconscious mind also. She has been presented all along as an extremely kind, sympathetic person but, when her closest friend, Lucetta, needs her most, she refuses to support her. Hardy says it is because she is very strait-laced and cannot accept any immorality but this explanation seems quite unconvincing. It is much more likely that her suppressed jealousy and humiliation have driven her to attack Lucetta's marriage to Farfrae.

What modern critics find most impressive is the way in which Hardy's characters, particularly Henchard, conform to the principles of modern psychology. It is all the more remarkable because it is purely the result of Hardy's observations on human nature.

POETIC ASPECTS

Another point that many modern critics emphasize is the fact that Hardy was a poet as well as a novelist (see John Holloway). Hardy himself preferred poetry to fiction. This had important results for his novels because he tended to think in poetic terms. He used poetic devices such as **metaphor** and symbolism extensively; this was unheard of for a novelist in Victorian times. Consequently, none of his early critics recognized what he was doing. (The same is true of Dickens. It was not until well into the twentieth century that George Orwell and Edmond Wilson pointed out that Dickens was also a symbolist.)

The use of symbols explains many other seeming coincidences and unbelievable occurrences. They were often meant to reveal something to the reader; rather than to be pure **realism**. The perfectly timed appearance of the furmity woman, for example, symbolizes Henchard's guilt returning to haunt him. The same is true of Newson's return. The effigy of Henchard which he finds in the river, is symbolic of his state of mind; his desire to kill himself. Symbolism is used to describe other characters as well as Henchard. When Hardy has Lucetta choose between two dresses, it is no accident that she picks the cherry-colored one. That color symbolizes her sensuality. There are innumerable such examples in the novel. In the opinion of some critics, there is almost too much symbolism. Hardy has a tendency to hit the reader on the head with his symbols so that they sometimes lose their effect. Having Newson return a second time to remind Henchard of his guilt, is one such example.

COMPARISON OF VIEWS AND AN EVALUATION

What Hardy is saying about life in the book, if anything, is another problem. The Victorian and post-Victorian viewpoint was that he was proving that virtuous people are rewarded in the end and unpleasant ones suffer. To them, the triumph of Farfrae and Elizabeth-Jane demonstrated that to have and practice the simple, old-fashioned virtues was the only way to happiness. To a large extent, Hardy did believe this. In all of his Wessex novels, he sets up a conflict between sophisticated, city-bred outsiders and the virtuous natives of Wessex; and, in

THE MAYOR OF CASTERBRIDGE

all of his novels, the simple, serious, usually proper natives are officially judged to be superior.

However, we feel today that Hardy was not quite convinced of this judgment himself. He disliked the extreme inhibition and hypocrisy that was typical of Victorian "niceness" and virtue as much as he disliked city ways. Consequently, he seems to have a hidden sympathy for characters like Lucetta, who may be somewhat immoral, but who are not afraid to follow their emotions. Certainly, to our eyes, Lucetta is far more appealing than Elizabeth-Jane for all her spiritual uplift and serious demeanor. To the Victorians, Lucetta was pure evil and Elizabeth-Jane pure good. Hardy's position was probably somewhere in between.

The comparison between characters is made in a different way between Farfrae and Henchard. Farfrae represents the modern Victorian world; proper, businesslike, mechanical, thrifty, and polite. Henchard has the lusty, rude, spontaneous spirit of the old-time country. He is a product of the period before the industrial age took hold in Wessex. Again, to a Victorian, Farfrae is obviously far superior morally to Henchard and so deserves to triumph. To us, Farfrae is colorless and unappealing. Hardy, we feel, is once more in the middle.

What we are left with, finally, is the idea that Hardy wanted to have his philosophical cake and eat it, too. His ideal of character was someone who was both virtuous in a conventional sense but natural and spontaneous at the same time. Unfortunately, the two were diametric opposites to the Victorians. This was a problem that Hardy could never resolve. He himself was basically a Victorian and it was impossible for him to stray too far from what he had been brought up to believe. He never really managed to create a satisfactory character who combined all the traits he admired.

Both Hardy's poetic techniques and his interest in psychology make him, to a degree, a modern writer. On the other hand, there is a great deal in his work which is completely Victorian. As a result of these two tendencies, Hardy stands in a middle point between such modern novelists as Gide and Conrad and such out-and-out Victorians as Meredith and George Eliot. *The Mayor of Casterbridge* is one of the first great modern novels and, also, one of the last great Victorian works.

qualities to greatness but also to self destruction - Ambition - honesty - competitiveness

THE MAYOR OF CASTERBRIDGE

ESSAY QUESTIONS AND ANSWERS

. . . .

Question: In what way can *The Mayor of Casterbridge* be considered a tragedy in the classical sense?

Answer: The construction of the novel closely resembles that of classical tragedy; especially in reference to the leading character. Henchard, as a tragic hero, fulfills the same requirements as do such figures as Macbeth and Oedipus. He is a great person than the others around him; this is shown by his ride from humble origins to the highest position in his society. Like them, also, this rise has been in many ways attributable to qualities which have led him to make great mistakes as well as to perform great feats. Like Macbeth, Henchard's ambition causes him to commit a great moral crime; one which can never be forgiven. Eventually, he is brought down by the repercussions of that act.

This, in itself, would not make him a tragic hero for it involves only external factors. It is his response to his guilt that really elevates him above ordinary mortals. Henchard, while admitting his guilt, struggles heroically against the fate which that guilt has brought on him. He struggles even when it is apparent that he cannot win. Finally, just as he has lost everything, he comes to understand the flaws in his character which caused so much suffering. It is this ultimate comprehension and repentance of his mistakes that makes Henchard truly tragic. He has committed great sins and he has suffered greatly for them but he has not been spiritually destroyed. In the end, he emerges purified; finally reaching an acceptance of his lot. Henchard leaves Casterbridge saying, "... but my lot is not more than I can bear," and he is speaking the truth. He has understood his life at last.

Question: Describe the function of the chorus.

Answer: The chorus in Hardy's works, as in Greek tragedy, is used primarily as a means of commenting on the action from a viewpoint different than that of the leading characters. In most cases, the chorus also conveys information to the reader in the form of opinions that would not come out otherwise. For example, we first hear of Henchard's doings in Casterbridge from the idlers in front of the King's Arms. From them, we get a very different picture of the mayor than we get from anyone else, or even from his own actions. We see how they hold him in great awe and are afraid of him but, at the same time, do not like him much and how they recognize his power over them but are resentful of it. Another example of their function as commentators is their opinion of Susan. They make it clear that they, and everyone else in the town, feel that Henchard has lowered himself socially by marrying her. We would not be at all certain of this without their comments.

In *The Mayor of Casterbridge*, more than in any other Wessex novel, the chorus has the additional function of outlining clearly the social structure of the town. They are definitely lower class and their relations with the major figures are important indicators of character. Henchard considers them his inferiors

THE MAYOR OF CASTERBRIDGE

and makes no bones about it despite the fact that he was once one of their class. The manner in which he treats them shows him to be extremely conscious of social position. This trait is, to some extent, responsible for his misfortunes; particularly in his first break with Elizabeth-Jane. Farfrae, on the other hand, is at ease with the chorus characters which points out his amiable ways and ability to make friends.

The other functions of the chorus are more commonplace. It adds comic relief and a dash of local color. Its members speak in dialect, make jokes, misuse words and expressions, make fools of themselves in general, reminisce about life in the old days, and so on. This serves to give the reader a break from the intense concentration on a single character, thus allowing him a chance to catch his breath and reflect on what he has been reading.

Question: What part does the conflict between "modern" and "traditional" attitudes play in the novel?

Answer: The first half of the nineteenth century in England saw the difficult transition from a pre-industrial, pre-mechanized Britain to "modern" Victorian times. In agriculture, the great changeover took place in 1846, with the repeal of the Corn Laws. This allowed the importation of foreign grain into England for the first time. Consequently, the entire structure and methods of British agriculture were drastically altered. As Hardy points out in his preface, most of the action in this novel takes place in the years immediately preceding 1846. These were the years in which the traditionalists made their last stand just before they were crushingly defeated in the name of progress.

The conflict between old and new is dramatized in the conflict between Henchard and Farfrae. Henchard is cast from the old mold. He is expansive, gruff, energetic; a man who has no use for records, who keeps his business affairs in his head. Farfrae is the opposite. He never takes risks based on anything but sound, calculated judgment; he keeps his books in perfect order; he uses the newest, most modern methods and equipment. The difference between the two men is summed up in their attitudes to the horsedrill. Henchard, like an old fogey, ridicules the new-fangled contraption. Farfrae correctly predicts that it will mean enormous progress for the farmers.

This disagreement is a kind of demonstration case of the insurmountable mental barriers between them. They cannot understand each other's business methods any more than they can understand each other's characters. They come from different worlds altogether. And since the old can never hold back the new for very long, Farfrae's association with modern and progressive ways is another symbolic indication that Henchard and his old-fashioned ideas are doomed to oblivion.

Question: To what extent is the setting important to the novel?

Answer: Unlike the other Wessex novels, *The Mayor of Casterbridge* takes place almost wholly in a rather sizable town; sizable at least for Wessex. This almost automatically means that the physical setting, so central in the other novels, cannot be nearly such an important force here. Casterbridge cannot be compared to Egdon Heath, for example; it plays a much smaller role.

The town does have some features which are important to the novel, however. These are mostly in the nature of symbolic reflections of mood and impressions. The very atmosphere of Casterbridge, dull and forbidding, evokes the age-old traditions of Wessex. Elizabeth-Jane remarks on its closed, narrow appearance when she first comes and this is a faithful description of its suspicious, conservative ways. The great antiquity of the town is demonstrated by its Roman ruins, which somehow seem actually to symbolize Casterbridge itself. There appear to be a great many hidden alleys and byways for such a small town, giving the impression that it is no stranger to plotting and intrigue.

The most powerful impression that the reader gets is one of timelessness. Hardy says that men had lived on its site 1500 years before and one can believe that little has changed in the way they live in all that time. Casterbridge, like all of Wessex, is accustomed to waiting. Twenty years is like a day to it, as Henchard discovers. It is the kind of atmosphere that does not allow anyone to forget anything; for it can wait as long as need to be punish the guilty.

Casterbridge, as an agricultural center, is important to the story. Its closeness and dependence on the country around it make it a perfect foil for the social pretentions of Henchard and Lucetta. When they forget their origins and become too self-important, something associated with the country or with nature always brings them down again; a rainstorm, a bad harvest, a crude peasant joke, or something similar. Thus, even in a town, one cannot escape the duty a person has to try to live in tune with nature.

Question: How can the assertion "character is fate" be applied to Lucetta?

Answer: Lucetta is a parallel to Henchard in many ways. She, too, has committed a sin in her past and she, too, tries and fails to rehabilitate herself. The reasons that she fails are to be found entirely in her character. She, even more than Henchard, is responsible for her own fate.

Lucetta's greatest failing is her vanity. In the long run, she thinks of no one but herself and her own happiness. If she had at any time thought of others, especially of Farfrae, her fate could have been avoided. For example, she could have told Farfrae herself about her past, as Henchard had suggested; but she does not tell him. She also might have saved herself had she treated Henchard with greater sympathy. In snubbing him, she herself sets in motion the events which finally cause her death. Even so, had she been less flighty and more tolerant of the townspeople, she might have escaped. Her high and mighty airs antagonize the lower classes, however, and they have no sympathy for her. It is significant that Longways and Coney warn Farfrae, but not Lucetta. As far as they are concerned, she probably deserves what she is getting and she will have to bear it as best as she can.

In the end, Lucetta herself recognizes that her vanity has destroyed her. Her last words are about the green parasol which the effigy is carrying. For a country town like Casterbridge, her green parasol is a perfect symbol of her snobbery. It is a sign to the world that she considers herself more sophisticated and worldly than the natives and, therefore, better.

The point is not so much that Lucetta is snobbish and vain about her appearance; other people are that. It is, rather, that she does not know where to draw the line or bother to consider the reaction of others to her ideas and her dress. She is weak and to be destroyed by this weakness is her fate. In that sense, she is even a better example of Hardy's dictum than Henchard for there are no outside forces working to thwart her. Her troubles are caused solely by her own flaws of character.

Question: Is Henchard a consistent character according to modern psychological knowledge?

Answer: Many twentieth century critics have marveled at the accuracy of Hardy's understanding of human psychology; long before anyone had ever heard of Freud and his discoveries. There is no doubt that Henchard is one of the greatest examples of a "complete" character in the modern sense. He has a subconscious life as well as a conscious one and both are perfectly drawn according to modern conceptions of the human mind.

As is true of everyone, most of Henchard's actions are perfectly rational and easy to understand: he acts in a certain way at a certain time because he is jealous, or because he is apprehensive of something, or for any number of other ordinary reasons. Such actions as these present no problem; however, some things he does are not so easy to comprehend. In these cases, when he seems to act without any sensible reason, his actions can only be understood in terms of his unconscious mind. If we are not aware of his subconscious motivations, we cannot grasp his character as a whole.

It is clear, for example, that, when he passionately showers Farfrae with affection the first time that he meets him, it is just that he is an emotional person, and that is his way of expressing himself. However, his even more passionate and fanatic drive to ruin the Scot later would be completely incomprehensible if we were not aware of Henchard's guilt feelings and the subconscious desire for self-punishment that they cause. Without realizing it himself, he actually wants to force Farfrae to fight him. His subconscious knows that he cannot win and this is his way of punishing himself.

There are many other instances of irrational behavior which can be understood best from this point of view. What is remarkable about Michael Henchard is that he represents, with great exactness, a kind of behavior not even described scientifically until the twentieth century. Yet no one, since Hardy, even in this century, has managed to create a more convincing psychological portrait of a man of this type. He is a perfectly drawn character, probably the finest individual character that Hardy invented and one of the greatest in all of literature.

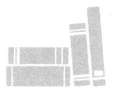

GLOSSARY

Bruckle - Unreliable, given to sudden changes.

Butter - firkin - A wooden vessel or cask for butter; also, a measure, usually one-fourth of a barrel.

Candlemas - The feast day of February 2nd commemorating the purification of the Virgin Mary.

Carrefour - A four-way intersection.

Chassez-dechassez - A French dance in which there is a great deal of movement across the floor.

Diement - Diamond.

Furmity - A thick drink consisting of kernels of wheat, raisins, spices and other ingredients stirred into boiling milk.

Gaberlunzie - Wandering beggar.

Gazebo - Balcony with windows commanding extensive view.

Gibbous - Hunched, humpbacked.

Hag-red - Harassed by supernatural beings, particularly witches.

Harry - a loud disturbance.

Hay-trusser - One who bundles hay in the fields.

Hontish - Snobbish; high and mighty.

Josephus - A popular work of history by Flavius Josephus, a Jewish historian.

Keacorn - The windpipe.

Kerseymere - A kind of woolen cloth.

Lammigers - Cripples.

Leery - Hungry.

Palladian - A style of architecture and design, originally Italian, introduced into England in the first half of the 17th Century.

Pembroke table - A table of four fixed legs and a number of additional ones which can be used to support hinged side segments.

Pis Aller - Makeshift; last resource.

Plim - Swell; become bloated.

Quagmire - Slang term for trouble.

Rummers - Large, circular drinking glasses.

Skimmity ride or Skimmington - A crude custom, common in the rural areas of England in the eighteenth century, designed to ridicule and embarrass adulterers. It consisted of a procession led by a donkey on which effigies of the offending persons were fastened. It was generally accompanied by much rude joking and noise-making.

Swailing - Boasting.

Skittle Alley - A straight runway for playing skittles; a game resembling ninepins.

Swipes - Poor quality or watered beer.

Tailing - The unusable part of grain; the refuse.

Victorine - A woman's fur scarf with long, narrow ends.

Wambling - Staggering; lurching.

Wheat-rick - A stack or pile of grain.

Wimble - An instrument for boring holes used in digging earth.

BIBLIOGRAPHY

Abercrombie, Lascelles. *Thomas Hardy: A Critical Study*. New York, 1912.

Beach, Joseph Warren. *The Technique of Thomas Hardy*. New York, 1922.

Blunden, Edmund. *Thomas Hardy English Men of Letters Series*, 1942.

Brennecke, Ernest. *Thomas Hardy's Universe*. New York, 1924.

Brown, Douglas. *Thomas Hardy*. London, New York, 1954.

Cecil, Lord David. *Hardy the Novelist*. Indianapolis-New York, 1946.

Chase, Mary Ellen. *Thomas Hardy from Serial to Novel*. Minneapolis, 1927.

Chew, Samuel C. *Thomas Hardy: Poet and Novelist*. New York, 1928.

Duffin Dr. Henry Charles. *Thomas Hardy: A Study of the Wessex Novels, the Poems and The Dynasts*. Manchester, 1937.

Elliott, A. P. *Fatalism in the Works of Thomas*. Philadelphia, 1935.

Firor, Ruth A. *Folkways in Thomas Hardy*. Philadelphia, 1931.

Guerard, Albert J. *Thomas Hardy: The Novels and Stories.* Cambridge, Mass., 1949.

Guerard, Albert J. ed., *Thomas Hardy. Spectrum Series*, "Twentieth Century Views," New York, 1963.

Hardy, Evelyn. *Thomas Hardy: A Critical Biography.* London, 1954.

Hardy, Florence Emily. *The Early Life of Thomas Hardy, 1940–1891.* London, 1928.

Hardy, Florence Emily. *The Later Years of Thomas Hardy, 1892–1928.* London, 1930.

Hawkins, Desmond. *Thomas Hardy.* London, 1954.

Hedgcock, F. A. *Thomas Hardy*, Penseur et Artiste. Paris, 1910.

Holloway, John. *The Victorian Sage; Studies in Argument.* London, 1953.

Lawrence, D. H. "A Study of Thomas Hardy," in *Phoenix*, 1936.

Lea, Herman. *Thomas Hardy's Wessex.* London, 1913.

Rutland, W. R. *Thomas Hardy: A Study of His Writings and Their Background.* London, 1938.

Southern Review, The vol. vi, 1940: "Thomas Hardy Centennial Issue."

Weber, Carl J. *Hardy of Wessex: His Life and Literary Career.* New York, 1940.

Weber, Carl J. *Hardy in America.* Waterville, Maine, 1946.

Webster, Harvey C. *On a Darkling Plain.* Chicago, 1947.